USBORNE
TRUE STORIES OF
D-DAY

USBORNE
TRUE STORIES OF
D-DAY

Illustrated by Ian McNee

Consultant: Terry Charman
Historian, Imperial War Museums

CONTENTS

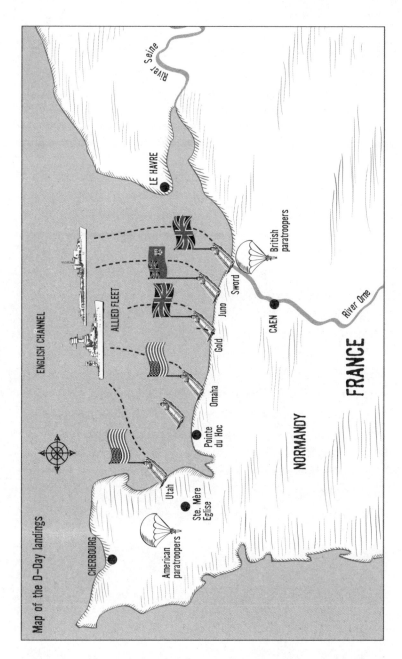

Map of the D-Day landings

ENGLISH CHANNEL

ALLIED FLEET

River Seine

LE HAVRE

British paratroopers

Sword

Juno

Gold

CAEN

River Orne

Omaha

Pointe du Hoc

FRANCE

NORMANDY

Utah

Ste. Mère Eglise

American paratroopers

CHERBOURG

A one-way ride into Fortress Europe

"If they attack in the West, that attack will decide the war."
Adolf Hitler, December 1943

In the end, it was the waiting that was the worst of it. For months, the soldiers had been herded from one isolated training camp to the next, forbidden to see their families and friends. The barracks and mess rooms buzzed with whispers: "when are we going, where will it be?" Everyone knew what was coming: the Allied invasion of Europe. They waited in the fenced assembly areas - nicknamed 'sausages' because of their bulging shapes on the maps of England - to be loaded onto transport ships. All through June 3, 1944, they waited away from the shore, huddled on the rain-lashed decks, seasick and apprehensive while the Channel seethed in the grip of an Atlantic storm. The largest seaborne invasion in history was kept waiting - all for a change in the weather...

Group Captain James Stagg was the man given the task of explaining the miseries of the English climate to General Dwight Eisenhower, Supreme Commander of the Allied invasion force. Stagg, a meteorological expert from the RAF, held twice-daily briefings on weather conditions across the English Channel. Described by Eisenhower as a *dour but canny Scot*, Stagg had disastrous news for the general and his fellow commanders that morning.

"A low pressure front has moved in from the Atlantic," he announced. "I expect tomorrow to be stormy, with strong winds, high waves and low clouds."

Eisenhower and the other commanders listened in dismay. Their troops were already embarked and waiting to begin the all-night journey across the Channel. Two years of planning had gone into the invasion mission - codename *Overlord* . In January the date for the attack, known as D-Day, had finally been set: June 5, 1944. But the generals were relying on calm seas and high clouds for any chance of success. In rough weather, the flat-bottomed landing craft carrying their armies to shore risked capsizing and, with low cloud, the Allies' control of the skies was no longer an advantage.

"When will conditions improve?" one general snapped.

"I can't say, sir," Stagg replied. "Our charts of the Atlantic are black with storms, moving in all directions."

"We could postpone for a day," Eisenhower proposed, turning to the other commanders to gauge their reactions. "But, after that, we'll have to bring the ships and men into port. It'll be at least two weeks before the tides and the full moon are right again. I'm not sure we can take the risk of our plans leaking out in the meantime. So, if we don't go tomorrow, we might have to cancel the whole operation."

After a brief discussion, the generals agreed to wait

for another 24 hours before standing down the invasion task force. D-Day was rescheduled for June 6 - provided the storm had abated.

"Group Captain Stagg," Eisenhower called to the departing officer. "When you come tonight, please try to bring me some good news."

On the face of it, the plan was simple. Take six army divisions - around 120,000 men - ship them across the English Channel to Normandy, and watch them fight their way through France and into the heartland of Germany. It was the British Prime Minister, Winston Churchill, who had selected the codename *Overlord* for the invasion. He asked to be taken along on the day, but the commanders refused, arguing that Churchill was too important for the 'war effort' to be put at risk. The Prime Minister stubbornly insisted he'd go anyway, as a regular seaman if necessary, until Eisenhower asked King George VI to intervene. "Well, if *you're* thinking of going, perhaps I'll come along too?" said the King to Churchill, knowing full well he couldn't possibly risk the safety of his monarch. So the Prime Minister stayed at home.

Churchill had been desperate to witness the strike into France. After the emergency evacuation of the British Expeditionary Force from Dunkirk in 1940, he had watched his hated opponent, Adolf Hitler, sweeping across Western Europe with his legions of stormtroopers. German armies made a series of spectacular advances into Yugoslavia, Greece, Russia and North Africa, until Hitler was able to boast that he had made Europe into his fortress. Under threat of invasion, Britain was almost cut off from the rest of the world, as her ocean trade convoys were savaged by fleets of enemy submarines, while the *Luftwaffe* - Germany's air force - pounded her cities with high explosives and incendiaries.

But, by 1942, the tide began to turn against Hitler. His offensive into Russia was crumbling and the defeat at Stalingrad in 1943 marked the beginning of retreat from the East. The mighty Afrika Korps, who had stormed across Libya to attack the British 8th Army, was decimated at the battle of El Alamein in Egypt. Germany's proud navy, the *Kriegsmarine*, was a spent force, and Hitler's beloved *Luftwaffe* was tattered and starved of engine fuel. The few squadrons that were still fit to fly were restricted to defending German airspace, in a desperate bid to safeguard the armaments factories. Hitler's Italian ally, Benito Mussolini, was deposed in 1943. His Japanese allies were contained within South East Asia and the Pacific. By early 1944, the once mighty divisions of the *Wehrmacht* - the German armed forces - looked worn and depleted after years of battle. The Russians were pressing in from the East, and the British and Americans were moving up through Italy and the South. It was time for the Allies to establish a new front in the west, and crush the forces of Nazi Germany once and for all.

For their landing point, the Allies chose an 80km (50 miles) stretch of the Calvados coast in the region of Normandy, France, a run of sandy beaches between the ports of Le Havre and Cherbourg. Their assault was divided into five beachheads: codenamed *Utah, Omaha, Gold, Juno* and *Sword*.

A great armada of minesweepers, destroyers, battleships and tank transporters would escort the soldiers across the Channel. Most of the infantry took passage in large troop ships, and were loaded into smaller boats for the journey to the shore. The British used 30-man LCA (Landing Craft Assault) boats, while the Americans provided thousands of *LCVPs* - Landing Craft Vehicle Personnel. LCVPs were also known as 'Higgins boats', after their designer Andrew Jackson Higgins. They were 11m (36 feet) long and 3m (10 feet) wide, and although lightly constructed from plywood and mahogany, they could carry 36 men or a jeep and 12 men. Cramped and unstable in heavy seas, Higgins boats looked like giant bathtubs. Their square bow was a single steel ramp that lowered

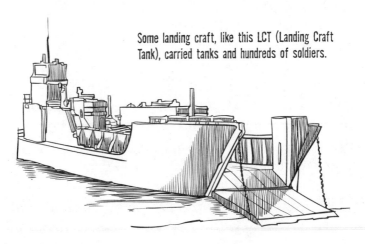

Some landing craft, like this LCT (Landing Craft Tank), carried tanks and hundreds of soldiers.

on landing. A whole platoon could charge across this ramp in seconds. Once it was raised, the Higgins reversed off the beach, ready to collect more men. The Americans made over 20,000 of these boats; the bulk of the Allied army in France arrived on one.

Military planners used standard army terms to describe the time and date of the invasion. *H-Hour* - the time the first men hit the sand - was planned for shortly after first light, at 06:30. From 01:00, on *D-Day* - an army expression meaning the day of attack - Allied planes would bomb the coastal fortifications. At H-Hour minus 35 minutes - 05:55 - the battleships would reinforce this with a bombardment of their huge naval shells. Landing on a rising tide, waves of infantry would stream up the beaches. (On a high tide, the German's underwater fortifications were still hidden, and on the low tide, there was too much exposed sand to run across.) Within two to three hours, the attackers would be battling their way inland, taking control of strategic roads, bridges and towns. To protect their flanks from enemy attack, three parachute divisions would deploy to the east and west, at around H-Hour minus three hours.

This was the simple plan. But it had two main problems: the logistics involved in shipping a whole army into a new battlefront in one day - and the impressive fighting potential of the German defenders.

Hitler described the Western European seaboard of his conquered territory as *The Atlantic Wall*. He appointed one of his most dazzling generals, Field Marshal Rommel, to protect it. It was a long frontier, and Rommel was only able to concentrate on certain key areas. He expected the invasion to start in Norway or around Calais, France, to take advantage of the short sea crossing from England. British intelligence services - the most capable in the war - encouraged him to think he was correct.

In *Operation Fortitude* the Allies used double agents and elaborate 'misinformation' tactics to keep some of the best soldiers of the *Wehrmacht* - and panzer divisions - stationed in Holland, Norway and the Calais area. Groups of British radio operators were sent to Scotland, where they filled the airwaves with phony messages about a phantom Allied army, poised to invade north of Holland. A Spanish double agent, codenamed *Garbo*, fed the enemy convincing reports about British preparations to attack in Calais. He was so trusted and admired by the Germans, they awarded him a medal: the Iron Cross. Acting on information from *Garbo*, Rommel committed his elite troops to the area around Calais. But the fortifications in Normandy were formidable too. Even though the strongest *Wehrmacht* divisions were guarding the wrong place, privately some Allied generals wondered if their own men would make it off the beaches alive.

The Germans had poured thousands of tonnes of concrete into a network of bunkers and gun emplacements stretching along the coast - all of it mixed and transported by hand and horse. They placed machine-gun posts, minefields, barbed wire and heavy artillery among the dunes. Work parties dragged specially constructed obstacles out onto the tidal flats. These included *hedgehogs*, giant crosses of welded girders, and *Belgian Gates*, 3m (10 feet) high fences designed to snag any landing boats. To make them even more deadly, most of these structures were draped with mines.

The defending soldiers were ill-equipped and badly trained, compared to the first-class crack troops around Calais. Many of them were old men or raw recruits, barely fit to fight. Some were downright hostile towards the Nazis. In their charge across Eastern Europe, the Germans had recruited political refugees and former POWs to serve in special *Ost* battalions. These men were treated almost like slaves, and only obeyed orders under the threat of harsh punishment. They grumbled about the poor food and the hard work, waiting for a chance to desert. But it would be wrong to dismiss the German forces in Normandy out of hand. Sprinkled among the low-quality troops were men with years of bloody experience on the Eastern Front. These combat veterans were particularly skilled in defensive tactics, and were determined to fight to the last man.

Their officers and generals had mixed feelings about the prospect of invasion, but all of them were anxious for it to begin. The *Wehrmacht's* last and only hope of winning the war was to smash the Allied armies in a fierce ground battle. Rommel was hindered by Hitler's neurotic insistence on maintaining control of the panzer divisions. The German high command was splintered and inefficient - unlike so many other features of their army - because of this meddling. But the *Wehrmacht* was still a powerful beast, prowling the length of the Normandy coast.

The Allies met the logistical challenges with gusto. Where a new boat was required for a specific task, they designed and built it. If the Germans dug anti-tank ditches - which, of course they did - the Allies fitted tanks with roll-up bridges to cross them. Allied scientists built other tanks with flailing chains, to clear routes through minefields, and equipped them with flame-throwers, to destroy the concrete machine-gun posts known as *pillboxes*. Engineers constructed two giant, artificial landing docks, called *Mulberries*, to receive supply ships in the days following invasion. *PLUTO* - PipeLine Under The Ocean - was an undersea cable, pumping vital fuel across the Channel.

The Allies' success at maintaining secrecy was no less impressive. Although hundreds of people knew the date and location of the invasion, it never reached the ears of the Germans. There was even a new level of security - higher than TOP SECRET. Anyone with knowledge of D-Day was classed as a *Bigot* by the British Secret Service. The information they possessed made them 'bigoted'. After a sudden attack by German *E-boats* (fast patrol launches) on ships taking part in an invasion exercise, 700 men were drowned. Among them were ten Bigots. The Allies were so worried that one of them might have been taken prisoner - and talked about D-Day - they sent divers down to recover the missing bodies. All ten *Bigots* were found and given military burials.

In another example of their security precautions, two workmen delivering and installing the maps of Normandy to army headquarters were detained as soon as they'd finished their work. They weren't released until June 7. Many in the UK played their part in the invasion - whether they knew it or not.

"Group Captain Stagg," boomed Eisenhower, late in the evening of June 4, "what do you have for us?"

Stagg had just entered the boardroom to give his report. He was smiling.

"A new weather front came in at midday, sir," he began. "The storm is clearing. It won't be perfect conditions, not by a long shot. But you should have pretty clear weather for June 6, with the clouds above two to three thousand feet."

"It's not what we were expecting," Eisenhower responded, deep in thought. Then he turned to General Montgomery, the commander-in-chief of the ground attack and the man who had defeated Rommel at El Alamein. "What do you think, commander?"

"I would say - GO," came Montgomery's bold answer.

Eisenhower deliberated for several more minutes, alone with the responsibility of launching the attack. At 21:45, he gave the order to proceed.

Operation Overlord was the world's largest amphibious invasion, involving millions of people in its planning and execution. Close to 175,000 fighting men were landed in one day, across a channel of stormy sea, supported by thousands of bomber aircraft, an armada of ships, fleets of tanks and supply vehicles. Churchill described it as, "the most difficult and complicated operation ever to take place."

But wars aren't won by operations or plans, no matter how impressive they might seem with hindsight. Victory or defeat is decided by the actions of small groups of one or two soldiers, in thousands of separate actions spread out across the battlefront. It might be a commando trying to destroy an enemy tank in a silent forest clearing; it could be an officer who risks his life to blow a hole in some barbed wire, so his company can escape a murderous gully on a beach. Or, it could be one man who is willing to charge a machine-gun post, to save a whole platoon.

Victory comes down to the initiative, bravery and the willingness to fight of individual soldiers. They inspire other men, and keep the army moving forward. It is their individual actions that make up the true story of D-Day.

Mr X meets the Desert Fox

The two men in the dinghy could hear the sound of a powerful engine drumming towards them across the waves.

"Maybe it's a Catalina flying boat, coming to rescue us," said George Lane, with a chuckle. His companion, Roy Wooldridge, wasn't amused. "It's a German patrol boat," he replied grimly. "They must have spotted us."

They were less than a mile off the Normandy coast, and the grey light of dawn was enough to make them easily visible from the shore.

"Throw all the kit overboard!" ordered Lane, quickly ditching their cameras and other reconnaissance equipment into the sea. "Let's hide our revolvers. If they think we're just shipwrecked sailors we might be able to overpower them and steal a ride home on their boat."

They stood up in the dinghy and waved their arms as the launch came closer. But, instead of pulling up alongside as Lane had hoped, the boat circled them. There had been reports of British commando raids along the beach the night before and the crew was suspicious of these castaways in their navy dinghy. A squad of soldiers ran to the prow of the launch and cocked their Schmeisser submachine guns, ready to fire.

Lane and Wooldridge glanced at one another, then dropped their guns into the Channel and raised their hands in surrender. Even the debonair Lane had a heavy heart. Their immediate future looked pretty grim;

although they'd been captured in their army battledress and should be treated as ordinary POWs, the Germans would want to know what they were up to, floating so close to the Atlantic Wall. They would certainly be questioned, perhaps tortured, then shot as spies. But, as it turned out, Lane would cheat the firing squad and have one of the strangest encounters of the Second World War.

George Lane was a commando officer, but you wouldn't have found his name listed on any official army document. Officially, Lane didn't exist. He was part of a secret unit of men who had taken on new identities, false names and family histories. Lane was a member of X-troop.

Ever since the Nazis came to power in Germany in 1933, they had carried out a systematic persecution of Jews, Romanies, and others they considered racially inferior, and refugees had begun fleeing the country. But, once war raged across Europe, the occupied nations found themselves scrutinized and categorized too. Fearing for their lives, thousands fled to neutral countries, or to Allied nations, especially Britain. Wanting to strike back at the Germans, many of these refugees tried to enlist in Allied armies, often in the face of official suspicion - sometimes even ridicule.

One senior commander who was receptive to the idea of establishing an 'alien' unit in the British forces was Lord Louis Mountbatten. He recognized the value of recruiting fighters with inside knowledge of occupied territories and fluency in the languages. (Mountbatten might have been influenced by the fate of his German-born father, Prince Louis Battenberg, who had been forced to resign from his post as First Sea Lord during the First World War, because of anti-German prejudice.)

In the spring of 1942, Mountbatten set up a new commando, No.10. They were known as Inter-Allied Commando, and like most commando units were composed of 10 troops, each with around 50 men. The troops contained Frenchman, Poles, Dutchmen and a host of other nationalities. But 10 Commando's strangest troop was made up of Jewish volunteers from Germany itself, or countries where German was the second language. Churchill described them as 'unknown warriors' and decided to call them X-troop, after the algebraic symbol for an unknown quantity.

The men of X-troop were expected to prove their loyalty to the Allied cause by taking on some of its most dangerous operations. In the middle of May 1944, Lane had been called to a secret meeting in Dover to discuss a covert mission to the Normandy beaches. He was ordered to lead a small group of engineers - known as *sappers* - onto the shore, and search for a new type of mine or explosive. British Intelligence suspected the Germans were installing this new weapon, following a freak incident a few weeks earlier. Bomber Command had made a daytime raid on some gun emplacements around Houlgate, a small town at the eastern end of *Sword Beach*. One of their planes dropped a bomb short into the surf, and the crew noticed that the blast had set off a chain-reaction of explosions all along the beach. Bombers often carried cameras to record their raids, and when photos of the explosion were shown to Mountbatten's scientific advisor, Professor J. D. Bernal, he was shocked by what he saw.

For months, the Allies had been monitoring, probing and testing German defensive lines in Normandy, until they believed they had identified every possible threat to the invasion. Their research had been exhaustive. In 1942, the British Admiralty had asked the public to send in photos, postcards and tourist brochures of the French coast. Hundreds of thousands of images poured in, and had to be sifted through by cartographers.

Eventually every cove, stretch of sand and beach-hut was mapped, then cross-referenced with aerial photographs of the region to construct accurate charts of the whole Normandy area. Admiralty staff consulted an array of scientists to explain the geological structure of the beaches and coastland. They sought out the most detailed written records available, discovering to their amazement that the work of Caesar's Roman surveyors during the invasion of Gaul was still useful. They even took sand samples, to establish whether or not the beaches could bear the weight of tanks. Major Logan Scott-Bowden and his 'midget-submarine' team made several trips to collect these samples. They became old hands at dodging German patrols as they scraped away at the dunes. Every model of mine and beach obstacle had been carefully examined and the Allies were sure they'd unearthed all the secrets of the German defensive capabilities. But the bomber photographs suggested otherwise. Perhaps the Germans had developed a mine that was detonated by vibration or magnetic attraction? If so, the invasion's landing craft might be at a greater risk than expected. The Allies had to know if such a device was buried on the Normandy beaches, so they sent X-troop to investigate. The expedition was known as *Operation Tarbrush*.

Lane could hardly have been a more exotic character. He was Hungarian by birth and his real name was Lanyi Gyorgy. Like all members of X-troop, he had taken a name that sounded English, but was similar to his own and easy to remember. If any X-troop commando was captured by the *Gestapo*, he would have to pretend to be a British soldier or risk identification, deportation and murder in a concentration camp. Lane spoke good English, but with a strong, lilting accent that baffled his superiors. They decided he should call himself a Welshman, in the hope that this would trick any interrogators.

Dashing and physically fit, Lane had been a water polo player for his country before the war broke out. He was already in England in 1939, studying at University, before dabbling in journalism. In 1943, he married Miriam Rothschild, a member of the British banking dynasty. His connections helped him enlist in the army and, on the strength of his abilities, he was rapidly promoted, until he won the right to wear the much-coveted green beret of a commando.

Eight *Tarbrush* raids were planned for the nights of May 15-18. The men were rushed across the Channel in a roaring MTB, a Motor Torpedo Boat. While the navy waited a few miles offshore, two commandos and two sappers took a *dory* - a small, powered boat - to within a few hundred yards of the beach, and made the last approach in silence, paddling a dinghy onto the sands.

The men had no idea what they were looking for - other than the fact it could be a mine. Normandy was littered with mines. Rommel had ordered his troops to lay over six million of them, all along the length of the Atlantic Wall. The defenders had a sinister variety to choose from. *Teller mines* were battlefield anti-tank charges that lay scattered all over the beaches; *S-mines*, or 'Bouncing Betties', as the troops called them, flew up a few feet before exploding, to cause maximum suffering to infantry; other mines had trip-wires, delayed fuses, and pressure catches. They came in a bewildering range of sizes and destructive capabilities.

Lane went ashore on May 15 and helped the sappers scan the beach with their metal detectors. All he found was a Teller mine that had been strapped to a stake, buried below the high-tide mark. He decided to recall his men and take it back to the scientists.

When he dropped the mine on the table back at base, the bomb experts were furious.

"You could have blown us all to pieces," they screeched. "It's unstable. Been underwater so long it's all corroded."

It was not a good start to the mission. Lane

returned on May 16, but a storm blew up and it was too rough to go ashore. On May 17 he went back for a third and final attempt, but his luck was about to turn sour.

Lane paddled in with his three-man team at around one in the morning and helped them unload their mine detectors. There was no need for him to leave the dinghy, as the sappers were carrying out the search, but Lane decided to join them in the reconnaissance patrol. He had an infrared camera with him, and was hoping to take some pictures of an anti-tank beach obstacle codenamed *Element C*.

When the party reached the dunes, the officers - Lane and Wooldridge - ordered the other men to drop back to the dinghy and stand guard, saying they'd return before three.

Only moments after the officers had stepped into the darkness, one of the men waiting by the dinghy saw a brilliant red flash among the dunes. There was a shout in German, then a terrible scream. Suddenly, a *star shell* flare exploded and the whole beach was flooded with light. The men hid the dinghy in the dunes, then ran to the water and swam out to their dory. Bullets were whizzing over their heads as they got its engine running and surged towards the MTB.

Lane and Wooldridge were still out on their moonlit ramble while all this was happening, and heard nothing of the beachside fracas. The first they knew of any trouble was when they doubled back to the dinghy and found it missing. Glancing along the beach, Lane spotted a German patrol. He hugged the sand, but the patrol must have noticed some movement. They immediately opened fire with their *Gewehr 41* assault rifles. In all the confusion, another patrol along the beach began returning fire. Lane and Wooldridge found themselves caught between two battling enemy groups. After a few minutes of keeping their heads down, they crept into the dunes and waited until their stretch of the beach was deserted.

Lane had a signal lamp and he flashed a message out to sea, hoping the MTB was lingering in the Channel. But the crew had already waited for the dory to return to shore and search for the officers, without success. The MTB was back in British waters, and there was only one hour left before dawn.

Pacing around, trying to think of a plan, Lane stumbled across the dinghy. The two men pushed it out beyond the breakers, hoping a current would carry them to some safe port. But in the morning they heard the rumble of the German motor launch approaching them. Under arrest and racing towards the shore, Lane wondered if his wartime adventures were finally over.

Once the prisoners reached the quayside, they were separated and locked in cold, underground cells without food or water. The first German interrogator walked into Lane's cell and asked politely: "You do know we're going to shoot you, don't you?"

It was hardly an encouraging start to the interview. Amazingly, Lane's Welsh cover story was believed and he concentrated all his energies on not reacting to the German he overheard - despite his fluency in the tongue. When the questioner fetched an interpreter, Lane had to go through the rigmarole of pretending he couldn't understand a word said between his captors.

Although he had removed the distinctive commando patches on his battledress, the Germans had carefully examined his clothes and could see the stitch marks.

"We know you are a member of the special forces," an officer said with a sneer. "And we have orders to shoot all captured commando saboteurs."

Thinking quickly, Lane explained that he wasn't a saboteur. He made up a story about being on a troop ship that had sunk in the Channel. The officer scoffed at this idea but was clearly intrigued. Instead of handing him over to *Gestapo* agents, he told Lane he would remain a prisoner of the *Wehrmacht*, the regular German army.

The interrogation went on for most of the day, with Lane sticking to his cover story. He was hungry and thirsty but his captors didn't maltreat him, despite being exasperated by his denials. Late in the afternoon, a man in a doctor's gown entered the room. Lane wondered if he was in for a new kind of treatment - he'd heard that crude, chemical 'truth serums' were used by some Nazi interrogators. But to his relief, the man only bound his wrists and blindfolded him.

The doctor must have been nervous or inexperienced, because he tied the blindfold too tightly. It was so taut across Lane's nose he could see down the gaps around his cheekbones. He was led out to a waiting staff car, where he saw Wooldridge sitting in the back. Lane was helped into the passenger seat and pretended to fall sleep. With his head tilted back, he could study the route the car took and keep a track of the French road signs they passed. It would be vital to know his location in the event of any escape attempt. The last sign Lane read before the car turned through some gates and started up a long drive was *La Petite Roche-Guyon*.

The two men were bundled out of the car and untied. When Lane's blindfold was removed he saw they were standing before a great castle, built into the side of a cliff. There was a forest all around, and trees thrusting out from the rock face, on a level with the castle ramparts.

Lane tried to exchange a few words with his fellow captive but the guards ordered the men to be silent and took them off to separate cells. The castle's prison facilities were luxurious compared to the earlier, damp dungeon, and Lane was even offered a cup of tea. When he was left alone for a few minutes, he checked his cell door and discovered it was unlocked. Stepping into the corridor, Lane came face to face with a huge Alsatian hound. He quickly changed his mind about making a run for it and went back to his cup of tea.

His next visitor was a high-ranking officer who spoke perfect English. He shook Lane's hand and asked how he was feeling. On hearing that Lane hadn't eaten for days, he called for some chicken sandwiches, much to the prisoner's delight.

"Now, if I were to introduce you to somebody I respect," the officer purred, "could I count on you to behave like an officer and a gentleman?"

Lane replied that he always acted like a gentleman, since he was one. He was immediately given soap and water to tidy himself up; the officer even provided him with a nail file.

He was led through a series of rooms until he reached a vast and opulently decorated ballroom. At the far end of the room, a slim man in a general's uniform was mulling over some papers. Lane had studied photographs of the German High Command and recognized the man at once. It was the master of the Atlantic Wall himself, Field Marshal Erwin Rommel, the legendary *Desert Fox*.

Lane was expecting Rommel to unnerve him by making his prisoner walk the length of the enormous room, but instead, the German master-strategist crossed over to meet his guest.

He was an impressive man, even at this late, weary stage in his military career. Rommel had fought for his country in the First World War, and had been awarded the Blue Max, Germany's highest military decoration. He had been a dynamic staff officer during peacetime, then emerged as one of the foremost panzer commanders of the Second World War, leading two divisions in Libya and Egypt - the feared *Afrika Korps*.

Rommel's sly but brilliant tactics earned him his famous nickname and a promotion to the rank of Field Marshal. At 50, he was the youngest German ever to hold the title.

During 1941-42, the Afrika Korps rampaged across the desert sands, almost striking as far as the city of Alexandria in Egypt. But there had been a string of defeats since then, and all that remained of the Afrika Korps panzer formations were piles of rusting scrap lying among the dunes. The glory days of the Desert Fox were long behind him, as he struggled to shore up the army's western fortifications. Though he worked himself into the ground for Germany, many of his army colleagues suspected he thought the war unwinnable. Because he rejected the crazed optimism of the Nazi leaders, his relationship with Hitler was often tense. If not an active participant, Rommel was at least aware of the army plot to remove 'the Fuhrer' that was gaining momentum in early 1944. It would eventually cost the Desert Fox his life.

Lane, Rommel, a few members of his staff and an interpreter sat down at an ornate table.

"So you're one of these gangster commandos?" Rommel began.

Lane countered this by saying he thought the commandos were the best soldiers in the world.

"So you are a commando?" sighed Rommel. "And a saboteur too, I suppose?"

Lane replied that he wouldn't have been invited to the castle if Rommel really thought he was a saboteur.

"You call this an invitation, do you?" Rommel snorted.

"Of course," replied Lane, through the interpreter. "But also a privilege," he added, with a smile.

Rommel hooted with laughter and Lane realized he'd broken the ice with the Field Marshal. They began to chat about Montgomery and his plans for the invasion, like two old friends meeting for a fireside chat. For 20 minutes, Lane managed to sustain a conversation with the man who knew more about the German positions in Normandy than anyone else. All the time he protected his true identity from the Field Marshal's cunning questioning.

"Where will the English attack come?" Rommel finally asked him.

Lane did his best to sound convincing when he answered that the best place for the British to land would be the closest point across the English Channel. Rommel seemed to agree with him and went on to discuss his wider thoughts on the war and the *Wehrmacht*'s occupation of France.

"The French have never been so happy in their lives," Rommel joked. "Their country runs perfectly."

Lane replied that he couldn't comment on this as he'd been blindfolded since arriving in France.

"That was an unnecessary precaution," Rommel snapped at his assistant. "I promise you will be fairly treated for the rest of your incarceration."

With this, Lane was cordially dismissed and returned to his cell, hardly able to believe what had just happened.

Wooldridge was also interviewed by the Field Marshal, but the audience only lasted a few moments. Perhaps he lacked Lane's impudence which seemed to amuse Rommel so much.

In keeping with Rommel's promise, both men were processed by the German authorities as regular POWs and treated well. When Lane finally arrived in his German prison camp towards the end of June, he was obliged to report to the English senior officer, Colonel Euan Miller. Realizing that Miller would never be taken in by his 'Welsh' drawl, Lane admitted to being a commando from X-troop on covert operations. The colonel was impressed by his story of meeting Rommel, and after he'd checked Lane's identity he managed to send a coded message out of the camp to his superiors back in England.

Lane had remembered the road sign he'd passed, close to the entrance to Rommel's HQ. Around July 17, the Field Marshal's staff car was strafed by a *Typhoon* fighter-bomber, and the driver was killed. Rommel was so badly injured in the crash he had to surrender his command. Three months later, he was implicated in a plot to assassinate Hitler, and offered the choice of committing suicide or standing trial for high treason. If convicted, his family would be ruined and disgraced, and all his financial assets would be seized. To safeguard his loved ones, he killed himself by swallowing a cyanide capsule.

There is no documentary evidence to prove whether the air strike on Rommel was a result of the information Lane provided to Miller, or simply a stroke of good luck for the Allies. But his meeting with the Field Marshal remains one of the most fascinating encounters of the war.

Lane was awarded the Military Cross for his services to X-troop. As for the mystery mines and *Operation Tarbrush*, army scientists decided the explosions along the beach must have been caused by unstable Teller mines. Perhaps they got the clue thanks to the rusty relic Lane had brought them, despite having trembled in horror at the time.

The Red Devils go to it

Major John Howard had always hated flying. On every training flight he'd ever taken, the 31-year-old Londoner made good use of his army-issue sick bag. But, for some reason, Howard hadn't suffered any nausea on this short flight across the English Channel. Perhaps he had too many other things to worry about, to be bothered by airsickness?

It was just after midnight, on June 6, 1944, and Howard was taking his men into combat for the first time in his life. He was in charge of six Horsa gliders, crammed with 150 paratroopers and 30 Royal Engineer sappers, due to crash-land in a muddy patchwork of French fields in only a few minutes' time. His orders were to seize two enemy bridges only five hundred yards apart, six miles inland from the Normandy beaches. After years of exhausting training and constant frustration at not being able to have a crack at the enemy, Howard was about to lead the very first strike of D-Day. It still seemed incredible to him, even though he'd known about his mission for several months, ever since his brigadier had summoned him to a confidential meeting at company headquarters.

"You must take these bridges *intact*," the brigadier told him, slapping his desk to emphasize the point. "A glider raid is the only way to do it. Land your forces right next to each bridge and overwhelm the Germans before they know what's happening to them."

"You mean a *coup de main* operation, sir?" Howard suggested. "A sudden strike?"

"Precisely," snapped the brigadier. "Hit hard and fast and don't fail me. The whole eastern flank of our invasion army could be at risk if you do."

"At risk from two small bridges?" Howard asked in amazement. "How can that be, sir?"

The brigadier got up from his desk and stepped over to the fireplace where a pile of logs was crackling away. He spoke quietly, staring intently into the blaze.

"The German army is still a formidable fighting machine. One of their greatest skills is organizing immediate counterattacks, even under intense pressure. There's a crack panzer division based at Cap de Calais, in the north of France. General Montgomery thinks they'll redeploy within hours of the invasion starting and make an assault. If those panzers rip into our eastern flank, they could push the landing force back into the waves."

"And these bridges," asked Howard, "are they the only route to the beaches?"

"They're one of the quickest," replied the brigadier. "That's why we need them. And the mastermind of Hitler's Atlantic Wall, Field Marshal Rommel, needs them too. Rommel's said that any beach landing has to be repelled quickly, or the battle for Normandy will be lost. He thinks the fight will be decided in one day. He even calls it *the longest day*, according to my intelligence sources."

"Then we'll do our best for you, sir," said Howard,

"Make sure you do," answered the brigadier, with a rare smile. "Now pick your men wisely, and make your plans..."

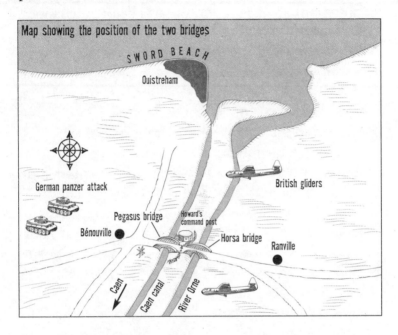

Map showing the position of the two bridges

SWORD BEACH

Ouistreham

German panzer attack

British gliders

Pegasus bridge

Howard's command post

Bénouville

Horsa bridge

Ranville

Caen

Caen Canal

River Orne

All around him in the cramped fuselage of the glider, Howard's No.1 platoon sang songs, chatted and chain-smoked. While his men tried to enjoy their last moments before going into battle, the major went over his plan of attack. He couldn't stop himself from checking it, as he had done a thousand times before, for any flaw or weakness. Howard knew it had to be perfect.

In a minute or two, the Halifax bombers towing the gliders would release their cables, and the assault group would be on their own over enemy territory.

The gliders would split into two groups, then crash-land next to their respective targets. After scrambling out of the aircraft, Howard's men had to rout the infantry entrenched around the area before the sappers could check the bridges for any demolition charges. The assault team was due to be relieved by a strong force from the 6th Airborne Division, landing at 00:50. It was a bold plan, the sort of mission that would make most soldiers tremble in their boots. But Howard and his men were no ordinary soldiers.

British paratroopers were the cream of that country's armed forces. Only the shadowy commando units could claim to rival them in fighting quality, but they operated outside the regular regimental system. Established as an elite division in 1942, by Major-General 'Boy' Browning, paratroopers were trained to be fitter and more resolute than the average soldier. A 'Para' always had his objective in mind and never swerved from it, no matter how tough the going. The regimental motto was a good illustration of this mental determination: *GO TO IT*. To make them distinctive within the armed forces, paratroopers wore a maroon beret - earning them the nickname *Rote Teufel* - 'Red Devils' - from German soldiers. Their uniform carried the symbol of the Greek warrior, Bellerophon, riding the mythical winged horse, Pegasus. These imaginative touches had been suggested by Browning's wife, the novelist Daphne Du Maurier.

Howard was a good example of the kind of man that made it into the Paras. He was from a large, working-class family where money had always been short, and had worked his way up through the ranks on merit alone. Ambitious and energetic, he led his men by example, joining them on the punishing cross-country runs and route marches that were part of everyday life in the regiment. It was a matter of personal pride that his men had been chosen for the raid and Howard had done everything possible to prepare them.

For weeks, the six platoons had been carrying out mock attacks on a specially constructed model in rural Devon. The bridge at Bénouville - codename *Pegasus* - had a detachment of 50 men. Five hundred yards to the east, Ranville bridge - codename *Horsa* - was less heavily defended and was surrounded by open country. Because of the threat of counterattack from the troops stationed in Bénouville itself, Howard intended to establish his headquarters at a pillbox on the east side of *Pegasus*, and keep the bulk of his force there. Each man knew his job inside out, and could take the place of any fallen comrade. The raid called for courageous leadership, and Howard had picked his platoon officers with great care, entrusting No.1 platoon - the first to storm *Pegasus* - to one of his closest friends, Lieutenant 'Den' Brotheridge. If all went well, the assault would be over in minutes, without the loss of a single man.

But Howard knew there were some risks that were outside his control. The German defenders were well-armed with Schmeisser sub-machine guns - known as *burp* guns by the Allies - hand-grenades, MG-42 heavy machine guns and, at *Pegasus*, a 50mm anti-tank gun. If they saw or heard the aircraft approach, they would blow them out of the sky. Bullets could easily tear through the plywood and cloth walls of a glider's fuselage, ripping into the unprotected paratroopers.

To fortify their positions, the Germans had laid a razor-wire perimeter around the fields next to the bridges. This was another reason why the gliders had to land so close to their target, to clear a path through the wire. There were other, more sinister threats to the mission. The enemy had planted tree-trunks and telegraph poles around key positions all over Normandy, linking them together with heavy cables. Some of the cables were primed with explosives. These poles, known as 'Rommel's Asparagus' by Allied soldiers, could rip the belly out of a glider before it even touched the ground.

But Howard's greatest worry had nothing to do with the Germans: it concerned his own men. They were untested in battle. How would they perform under fire, when a second's hesitation or panic could mean death? There was no way of knowing how they - or Howard himself for that matter - might react to the shock of combat. But the commander placed all his trust in his men and his training. All the same, like so many other soldiers going off to war, he carried a good luck charm. The gruff major, dressed in battle fatigues and with camouflage paint smeared over his face, had a tiny, leather shoe hidden in one of his pockets. It belonged to Terry, his two-year-old son.

At 12:07 the gliders dropped their towlines and got into formation, each group of three flying in sequence, one minute apart. The men stopped singing, retreating into their own private thoughts as the pilots banked and turned, searching for their targets.

At 12:14, there was a shout from the cockpit of the first glider: "Get ready. We're on the approach."

Staff Sergeant Jimmy Walwork of the Glider Pilot Regiment was trying to keep his course straight, aiming directly for the silhouette of a low bridge looming up a few miles ahead. With no propeller power, over-burdened and at the mercy of the summer air currents, the glider was almost impossible to control. Howard was sitting at the front of the aircraft, and could see the sweat dripping off the pilot's forehead as he struggled with the joystick. In the eerie silence of the night, everyone waited for the touchdown, and the immediate thunder of enemy gunfire they expected to accompany it.

As soon as the undercarriage hit the ground, Walwork knew he was going too fast. "Stream," he yelled to his copilot, indicating that they would need the emergency parachute to bring the glider to a halt. There were so many sparks and flashes coming from the landing 'skids' as they scraped across the earth, the paratroopers thought they were already under fire. Their glider bounced back into the air, then came to ground with a huge crash, as the nose section plunged through a wall of razor wire and stopped dead. The halt was so sudden, both pilots were launched through the glass front of the glider and landed, unconscious, in the lush, Normandy grass.

Howard was convinced he'd been injured in the crash; he was deaf and blind. His head ached, there was total silence and he was in darkness. Soon, he heard the other paratroopers around him stirring, groaning, and checking their bodies for cuts and broken limbs. His hearing was fine - but where was the gunfire? Surely, the Germans must have heard the crash? Why hadn't they opened up with their MG-42s? With his heart racing, Howard gingerly raised his fingers to examine his eyes, only to discover that his helmet was rammed down over the bridge of his nose. When the glider bounced he must have been thrown up against the fuselage and hit his head. With a sigh of relief, he punched the helmet off his brow and found himself staring out at the night sky. The glider doors had been ripped off on landing and Howard watched Brotheridge's platoon staggering out into the moonlight, assembling for the attack. Only fifty yards away, towering over a line of trees, the steel girders of *Pegasus bridge* stood waiting.

In a display of piloting brilliance that was later described by the Commander of the Allied Air Forces as "one of the most outstanding flying achievements of the war," Jimmy Walwork had landed them 'on the button' within sight of the target.

Only seconds later, Brotheridge called, "Come on men," and led his platoon out of the field and over an earth embankment. The lieutenant was a powerful, athletic 26-year-old. His friends thought he'd become a professional soccer player when the war was over. Screaming a battle cry that cut through the night, he waved an arm for his men to follow and sprinted towards the bridge.

Private Helmut Romer, a 16-year-old novice soldier, was one of two German sentries guarding *Pegasus* that morning. He had heard the thud of something crash into a field, but thought it was part of a damaged enemy aircraft or an unexploded bomb falling to ground. After months of Allied air attacks, he didn't pay much attention to every strange noise he heard on duty. But if Romer didn't trust his ears, he couldn't doubt his eyes. His mouth fell open as he saw more than twenty British paratroopers charge out of the trees. While three of the raiders turned off to attack the pillbox with grenades, Brotheridge led the others across the bridge, yelling their platoon cry, "ABLE, ABLE," at the top of their lungs. They had blackened faces and wore full camouflage dress; their lightweight, *Sten* sub-machine guns came to life as they opened fire on the defenders.

Romer knew he was no match for the feared Red Devils. So he turned and ran. The other sentry was tougher; he managed to keep his nerve long enough to fire a warning flare into the sky. As the sleepy Germans in the trenches saw the flare and realized they were under attack, the second glider smashed into the field, only yards from the first. Lieutenant David Wood gathered his men and rushed in to join No.1 platoon.

Brotheridge and his troop were fighting their way across the bridge, hurling grenades and firing from the hip. Most of the German defenders were too stunned or terrified to put up a fight, but some of their officers were veterans of the Eastern Front. They came to their senses, firing their Schmeissers at the attackers and running to man the 'nests' of heavy machine guns.

As Brotheridge reached the western end of the bridge, he saw some movement in the nest to his right and he tossed a grenade over its sandbag wall. Before it could explode, a burst of machine gun fire hit him in the neck. He was lifted off his feet by the fusillade, and slammed down onto the road, mortally wounded. The battle raged around him as he lay dying, the first Allied soldier to be killed by enemy fire on D-Day.

That moment, the third glider arrived, landing just north of the other two. It was another sudden stop, and Lieutenant 'Sandy' Smith shot out of the front of the aircraft and found himself stretched out on the grass, staring up at the stars.

"Well," said one of his men, rushing over, "what are you waiting for, sir?"

Smith struggled to his feet and, despite the shock of the crash-landing, plunged into the battle. His platoon had orders to assist Brotheridge and secure the western approach to the bridge. With small-arms fire buzzing all around them, Smith drove his men forward. As he reached the end of *Pegasus bridge*, he noticed a German soldier leap up, poised to throw a grenade. Smith managed to shoot him down with a blast from his Sten gun, but the grenade landed at his feet and he was caught in the blast.

When he'd dusted himself down, Smith saw that his trigger finger was hanging by a thread of skin and there were deep gashes all over his hands. Ignoring the pain, he pushed forward, firing bursts from his gun with his second finger and shouting encouragement to his men as they struggled onward. Smith was later awarded the Military Cross for his courage.

By now, the battle was drawing to a close, but still there were pockets of stubborn German defenders. At the eastern end of the bridge, Lieutenant Wood took three bullets in his leg from a sniper and crashed to the ground in agony. All three platoon officers had now been hit, but the bridge belonged to the paratroopers.

At 00:22, Major Howard set up his headquarters in the captured pillbox. The bridge was his and, apart from the odd sniper shot, there was little enemy activity. A captain from the sappers reported that the area was clear of explosive charges and booby traps. In fact, the commander of the bridge garrison, Major Hans Schmidt, had ordered them to be removed because he was convinced there was no threat of attack. He was more worried about accidents or sabotage by the French resistance. The first phase of the mission was accomplished, but there had been a heavy price to pay. Howard's No.2 and No.3 platoon leaders were severely wounded, and Den Brotheridge was dead. Controlling the emotions he felt at the loss of his friend, Howard waited for news from *Horsa bridge*, and the fate of his No. 4, 5, and 6 platoons.

But the landings around *Horsa bridge* had not gone smoothly. At 00:20, Lieutenant Dennis Fox, commanding No.6 platoon, came down 300 yards from his target. The two gliders that were supposed to precede him had drifted off the landing zone. Lieutenant Todd Sweeney and No.5 platoon came down half a mile away, while Lieutenant Tony Hooper's No.4 platoon landed eight miles off-target. Even though his platoon was alone Fox didn't hesitate to attack. The German defenders could hear the rattle of gunfire at *Pegasus* and were already alerted to the imminent attack. A long burst from an MG-42 almost stopped them, but Sergeant 'Wagger' Thornton, according to Fox the platoon's most capable man, was ready with a light mortar - a portable cannon. An expert shot, he scored a direct hit on the machine gun nest and Fox was able to resume the attack.

As No.6 platoon stormed the bridge, screaming "FOX, FOX," and emptying their Sten guns, the German defenders jumped out of their trenches and ran into the night. By 00:26, Howard had news on his field radio that *Horsa* was secured. He ordered Fox and his platoon to wait for No.5 platoon to dig in then join the defenders at *Pegasus*. Sweeney's men in No.5 had arrived moments after the attack and were rather disappointed to miss out on the fight. With both bridges captured, the greatest threat to Howard's mission was a counterattack from the Germans in Bénouville. According to intelligence reports, there was even the possibility that the garrison there had a number of panzers - and the paratroopers were only lightly armed. Howard estimated his reinforcements from 6th Airborne would arrive by 01:00, but he was well aware that these men could be delayed; high winds and inaccurate navigation were the curse of many D-Day parachute missions. If an attack came before the relief force reached them, Howard's men would simply have to hold their ground.

The first skirmish wasn't at *Pegasus*, but at the eastern end of *Horsa*, when Sweeney's men shot and killed a passing enemy patrol. Minutes later, they ambushed a staff car that was racing towards the bridge. The passenger turned out to be none other than Major Hans Schmidt, returning to base after enjoying a night out with his French mistress. His injuries were treated carefully, despite his ranting about 'the mighty Fuhrer' and the general hopelessness of the paratroopers' situation.

At 01:00 there was still no sign of the reinforcements. Howard sent Fox and his platoon to take up positions around the road junction leading onto *Pegasus* at the Bénouville end.

"You'd better take a PIAT with you," he warned his officer. "Our guests will be here soon."

There was already a steady rumble, like approaching thunder, coming from the heart of the town. The Germans were warming up their panzers for action.

At 01:30, Fox and his platoon noticed a tremor in the earth beneath them. The sound of engines and shouts was getting louder, and suddenly they saw the menacing shape of a panzer lurch out of the darkness along the road. Two other tanks and a body of infantry followed in the rear.

"I think you're the man for the job," Fox whispered to Sergeant Thornton, sending him forward with the PIAT. With every nerve tingling, Thornton dropped into a trench and took aim at the lead tank. It was a Panzer Mk. IV, 24 tons of hardened steel, rumbling towards the bridge at walking speed. Thornton carefully adjusted the sights on his PIAT. This was the only weapon the paratroopers carried that stood a chance of stopping a tank.

The *Projector Infantry Anti-Tank* was the British version of the American infantry's bazooka. It was powerful but difficult to load and could only penetrate the thick hull of a panzer at short range. Thornton knew that if he missed, or if the PIAT shell bounced off the tank's steel plates, there would be no time to reload. As soon as he revealed his position, the tank's machine gunner would cut him down. If Thornton missed, the panzer would force his fellow paratroopers from the bridge, and the Germans would have a clear road all the way to the Normandy beaches. The sergeant could feel the sweat breaking out across his back as the tank pushed relentlessly towards him. He only had seconds to play with, to make the most important shot of his life.

Waiting until the last possible moment, Thornton fired a shell 'point-blank' into the side of the panzer and watched it explode into flames. It was a hit. The blast set off a chain reaction, as the shells and ammunition loaded inside the tank began to detonate. For twenty minutes the area around the panzer was a fireball, lighting up the sky. The other Germans thought the explosions were all the work of the enemy, and decided they must be facing a large, heavily-armed force. Their commander ordered an immediate retreat.

A few minutes later, the first reinforcements arrived. Captain Richard Todd, a promising young actor who had abandoned his stage career to fight for his country, was among them. He would later play the role of Major Howard in the film *The Longest Day*.

With the arrival of his relief force, John Howard's mission was accomplished. General Montgomery later presented him with the DSO, the Distinguished Service Order, for his bravery on D-Day. In a few hours, the Normandy landings would begin, without any risk of panzer attack from the east. The Red Devils had scored the first victory for the invasion, and proved their mettle beyond any doubt.

Precious metal on Gold Beach

Stanley Hollis was the landlord of *The Green Howard*, a quiet public bar in the small town of North Ormesby. Stanley was a modest, easy-going man with patient eyes and the hint of a smile always playing across his lips. He seemed content with his lot in life. His wife and two children lived with him in the rooms above the bar and, if they were happy and well-provided for, Stanley was at peace. On busy nights, the whole family helped to serve thirsty customers. Stanley was proud of his children, and proud of being a good landlord. If you didn't know any better, you might have thought he'd done the job all his life.

But Stanley had seen a lot more of the world than the four walls of a 1960s bar. He'd been a soldier and his body bore scars from grenades, mortar shells and machine gun rounds. When he'd been standing for a few hours, serving drinks, the old wounds in his feet opened and bled. There were German bullets still lodged in his bones. He had splinters of bomb shrapnel trapped in his arms and there was a silver plate mounted in his skull, a memento of emergency battlefield surgery.

Stanley had another metal keepsake. Hidden inside a drawer behind the bar, lying among discarded bottle tops, balls of string and household clutter, he kept a bronze medal. It was a Victoria Cross, the highest award for bravery a British soldier can receive. The late

King George VI had pinned the medal to his uniform in a ceremony at Buckingham Palace in October, 1944. Even in the exclusive world of VC winners, his achievement was a remarkable one. His bravery had been exceptional *twice* on the same, momentous day, while fighting alongside the best soldiers the Allies could put into battle. Stanley was the only man

The Victoria Cross

to win a Victoria Cross on D-Day. The quiet landlord with the gentle smile was one of his country's greatest war heroes.

Stanley Elton Hollis had been a 23-year-old sergeant major on the morning of the Normandy invasion, waiting with his platoon on the lurching decks of an Allied troopship. He had earned his promotion from the ranks of the Yorkshire regiment, *The Green Howards*, after four years of bitter fighting. Hollis had been at Dunkirk in 1940, when the British Expeditionary Force was driven out of Europe by the might of the German *Wehrmacht*. During the evacuation, he distinguished himself by going to the aid of a platoon of Welsh Guards infantry who were almost surrounded by the enemy.

Stationed in North Africa in 1942-3, Hollis fought Rommel's elite *Afrika Korps* at the battle of El Alamein. In Sicily he was recommended for a Distinguished Conduct Medal for courage under fire. (It was never awarded, due to a communication mix-up in the confusion of war.) Hollis had been seriously wounded four times, but on each occasion forced himself to recover, anxious to rejoin his friends in the regiment. Although he had become something of a Green Howard talisman - and a hero figure to the raw recruits under his command - the sergeant major never let it go to his head. He was as scared of being injured or killed as the next man, but this didn't stop him from doing everything he could to help win the war.

Hollis was born in Middlesborough in the north of England and had drifted through a series of casual jobs and a stint in the merchant navy before signing up with the Green Howards on the eve of conflict. He was proud of his regiment and their 300-year tradition, and counted his fellow soldiers as his closest friends. Throughout his war service, he had tried to protect or rescue other men from danger. Unlike some people who earn a reputation for daring, Hollis never risked the lives of other soldiers for personal glory. His men stayed close to him, knowing he would use his fighting skills and experience to protect them.

'Virgin' soldiers often feel reassured by the calm presence of a veteran. It was no different on board the troopship, *Empire Lance*, as novice Green Howards clustered around their sergeant major. Every man sensed the challenge ahead. They were seven miles off the coast of Normandy and could just make out their target, *Gold Beach*, a forbidding grey blur across the choppy waves of the English Channel.

"Get your kit together," Hollis ordered gruffly. "Pick it up, pack it, check it over, then check it again."

He knew he had to make his men concentrate on the simple tasks of testing their weapons and equipment, rather than dwell on their chances of survival once they reached the shore. Around 500 soldiers from the Green Howards were going in as part of the first attack force on *Gold Beach*. They were due to land at 'H-Hour' - 06:30 - and had already been up for three hours, preparing for battle, after a breakfast of fried eggs washed down with a shot of navy rum.

Their mission was to capture and disarm the Mont Fleury battery, a network of concrete casements with heavy guns that threatened the invasion fleet. This target was defended by pillboxes, barbed wire and minefields; the Green Howard officers knew they'd been given a tough nut to crack. They had been warned to expect heavy casualties - perhaps 70% of their men dead or wounded.

"Over you go," called Hollis, when the signal to disembark finally came, shortly before dawn. "Mind yourselves on those scramble nets."

Peering over the side of the ship, the soldiers studied the flat-bottomed landing craft bobbing violently on the waves. The sea was still rough after the storm the day before, and each wave crest lifted or dropped these troop barges a good ten feet. Weighed down with guns, ammunition, food rations and all their other kit, the men risked being crushed against the steel hull of the troop ship as they slowly worked their way down the special rope webbing. It was a nerve-wracking descent. Even the strongest swimmers knew they'd have no chance of staying afloat if they lost their footing. When the platoon of 20 was all safely on board, Hollis breathed a long sigh of relief as the LCA surged away.

For the next 45 minutes, they circled, waiting for the other boats to load up. The LCAs rocked violently and the bulk of the men quickly started to feel seasick. By the time they were lined up and ready to begin the journey to the shore, the boats stank of vomit and sweat. Every few seconds a wave would crash over the side, drenching every man to the skin. The water was so cold it made their cheeks and fingers numb and the salt burned their eyes. Some men suffered so badly with the motion sickness, they thought they'd die before they reached dry land. It would take more than an hour for their boats to reach the Normandy sands.

Before they were halfway in, the Allied fleet behind them began a massive shore bombardment. For forty minutes, the huddled men watched as huge shells tore across the sky, smashing into the coastal fortifications. Soldiers later described it as sounding like freight trains crashing past. Their explosions shook every man to the core.

But the ship-to-shore blasting was only part of the Allied barrage. Hollis watched thousands of rockets launched from floating platforms that had been towed across the Channel. He craned his neck to scan the squadrons of bombers droning overhead. These planes carried huge, concrete-busting bombs designed to smash through the Atlantic Wall. The Normandy coastline burst into fire, and a curtain of flames hundreds of feet high raced out to the far horizons. It was a breathtaking sight. The inexperienced men in the platoon were convinced that nothing would be able to survive it. But Hollis and the other veterans knew better. The German defenders were hiding deep underground, safe in their steel-reinforced concrete bunkers. Seconds after the shelling ceased, they would be racing to the surface to prime their guns.

As the platoon chugged towards the beach, Hollis spotted what he thought was a pillbox set back on the dunes (although hours later he discovered it was only a crude rain shelter). Fearing his men would be cut down by an MG-42 as soon as they landed, he grabbed a machine gun and started blasting at it. That moment, the Allied fleet's bombardment stopped and the landing craft started to come under fire from the dreaded 88mm German guns and light mortars. The Royal Navy coxswain, or boat pilot, revved the LCA engine to get closer to the beach and Hollis stopped shooting, ready to jump out with his troop into waist-high water.

He thought it would be a good idea to take the gun with him. Without hesitating he seized the barrel. But it was still red-hot. Hollis snatched his hand away and watched a blister lifting on his palm, as big as a finger.

He later described this as one of the most painful wounds he suffered in the war, but there was no time to treat the burn. The next moment, the landing craft ramp crashed down and the platoon charged forward. One of Hollis' good friends, Sergeant William 'Rufty' Hill, was among the first out. He took one step off the ramp and vanished underwater. Some of the naval shells had fallen short, leaving deep craters hidden beneath the surf. Before Hill could ditch his heavy equipment and swim to the surface, the landing craft lurched forward on a breaking wave. Hill, a survivor of the battles of Dunkirk and El Alamein, was cut to pieces by its propeller blades. He wasn't the only man to die before setting foot on French soil.

But there was no time for the platoon to mourn the loss of their friends. They were exposed and vulnerable as they waded towards the beach, and Hollis did his best to keep them moving. Although the weight of enemy fire was less than the Green Howards had anticipated, it was essential to get out of the 'killing zone' around the breaking surf. This area was already marked by burned-out tanks and dead and dying men.

When they reached a ridge at the top of the beach the platoon set up two Bren machine guns and some light mortars to launch smoke canisters. It was their job to lay down smoke and covering fire across a minefield that ran up between some dunes. This was the Green Howards' pathway to the battery. Hollis watched as a group of sappers inched forward to clear the mines, laying a white tape behind them to indicate where it was safe to tread.

As soon as two platoons were assembled to make the attack, the Green Howards scrambled across the minefield and began to climb through scrubland to their target. Hollis followed with his own platoon and a senior officer, Major Ronald Lofthouse. As they worked their way up a hill, Hollis suddenly saw the advance party come under machine-gun fire. They were pinned down, and couldn't see where the rounds were coming from. Lofthouse and the sergeant major crawled to the top of the hill and studied the terrain. After a few seconds, Lofthouse spotted a mound of concrete, camouflaged in the scrub.

"There's a pillbox over there, Sergeant Major," Lofthouse whispered.

Hollis followed the officer's gaze until he detected the stronghold, only yards away. He could see the muzzles of the German guns traversing in thin slits in the concrete shell. They were MG-42s.

The German MG-42 heavy machine gun, nicknamed the *Spandau* by Allied soldiers, was a fearsome weapon. Versatile and reliable in the worst conditions, it was immensely powerful, spitting out 1,200 rounds of ammunition per minute in a distinctive 'sheet-ripping' growl that every Allied soldier learned to recognize. Unlike most of the American and British weapons, there was no muzzle-flash or smoke released from its barrel. This made it difficult to locate on the battlefield. With no warning, an MG-42 could spit out hundreds of bullets in a matter of seconds. Advancing against this firepower was a real test of courage. Tackling an MG-42 on your own was little short of suicidal.

Hollis took his Sten gun, clambered up onto his feet and charged at the pillbox.

It must have been an incredible sight for the pinned-down soldiers of the Green Howards. One of their own men was sprinting across the sand, weaving and ducking, firing bursts from the hip - alone against a fortified machine-gun post. The German gunners must have been startled too. They fired on Hollis, nicking his ear and grazing an eyebrow, but they couldn't knock him down. In a few seconds, he'd reached their position and clambered onto its concrete roof. He crouched over and flipped a grenade through the gun slit, then jumped to the back of the pillbox. There was a muffled boom, followed by desperate shouts. The dazzled German survivors poured out into the sunlight, where Hollis took them prisoner. As he was rounding them up, he noticed a trench running towards another concrete bunker. Hollis rushed at it, slipping a fresh magazine into his Sten. The defenders in the other pillbox hadn't been expecting an attack from behind. Convinced that they'd been outflanked by a whole platoon or more, they came out with their hands in the air.

Hollis took around 18 prisoners in his solo assault, clearing the way for his company to seize the battery. It was an amazing act of selfless bravery, and won him a recommendation for the Victoria Cross.

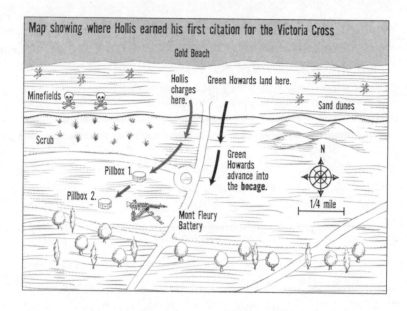

Map showing where Hollis earned his first citation for the Victoria Cross

But Hollis wasn't just a one-shot hero. Only a few hours later, he received his second nomination for the medal, for another act of incredible courage.

By noon of D-Day, the Green Howards had secured most of *Gold* Beach and were advancing into the Normandy countryside - known as *bocage*. This rolling landscape of small fields separated by high hedgerows and woods had been cultivated by French farmers for generations. From the air it looked like good terrain for advancing infantry. But, in one of the major blunders of *Operation Overlord*, the *bocage* turned out to be a nightmare for the Allies.

The hedgerows were a deathtrap. Thick and thorny, growing on solid earth banks four feet high, they were almost impenetrable. Some were so old, the hedges had curled and meshed together at the top. Stepping into one of these lanes was like entering a long, green tube. Soldiers had to blast holes in them with grenades if they wanted to clear a gap. Even tanks had trouble smashing through. They could get stuck between the steep earth banks. By setting up their MG-42s or antitank guns at strategic crossroads or gateways, two or three German soldiers could hold off a whole company of attackers. It might take a day of fighting to gain a few yards along these thin lanes that snaked all over the Norman countryside. The villages and lone farmhouses dotted among them made ideal strongpoints for the enemy. They lay hiding in the ruins, or lurking in the shadowed glades.

Hollis had been ordered to take his platoon and scout around the village of Crépon, clearing the way for his battalion. To the west of the village, Hollis spotted a solitary farmhouse and he went over to investigate. The building was deserted - apart from a young boy hiding upstairs - but when he glanced around the rear garden wall, a bullet exploded in the stonework next to his ear. A German sniper had missed him by an inch. Hollis fell backwards, wiping blood from his eyes. His face was a mass of cuts, peppered with stone shards from the wall.

Ignoring the pain, he gingerly peered around the wall and saw a hedgerow running along the top of a field of planted rhubarb. A couple of dogs were barking at a break in the hedgerow and Hollis thought he could just make out the shape of an artillery piece.

It was a German gun squad, ready to ambush his battalion.

He rushed back to Crépon and reported to Major Lofthouse.

"You'd better hit them with a PIAT, Sergeant-Major," Lofthouse ordered. "Take a couple of machine gunners with you to cover your retreat."

Hollis started back to the farmhouse with two soldiers equipped with Bren guns. The Bren was the main machine gun for the British infantry, with a powerful but slow rate of fire. It could be used as a fixed position weapon or fired from the hip - if a soldier was strong enough to handle it.

When the three Green Howards reached the farmhouse they got down on their bellies and began crawling through the field. The rhubarb was so bushy they soon lost sight of each other, but Hollis could hear the other two rustling along beside him. When he was close enough to get a shot off, he took careful aim and pulled the trigger. The PIAT bucked in his hands and he watched the shell scream towards the German position - and miss.

The next instant the Germans' gun roared and a shell skimmed over the rhubarb field, exploding inside the farmhouse. Hollis cursed his poor aim and called out to his men to fall back. Then he crawled to safety under a cloud of dust and falling debris.

When Major Lofthouse heard about the failed attack, he decided to reroute the battalion around the village, to bypass the ambush. "We're in a hurry," he barked. "I can call in an air strike to deal with it later. Wait a minute, though. What's all that noise?"

There was a rattle of gunfire coming from the ruined farmhouse, the unmistakable snarl of Spandaus. Lofthouse stopped a soldier who was rushing by. "What's happening up there?" he demanded.

"There are two Bren gunners trapped in a field," the man explained. "The Germans spotted them and now they can't budge."

"Those are your men, Sergeant Major," cried Lofthouse.

"I know, sir," Hollis answered. "And as it was me who took them in, I'll be the one to bring them out."

Hollis armed himself with a Bren and sprinted over to the farmhouse. He could see the Germans scouring the field with machine gun fire, trying to flush out the two soldiers. Any second now, their bullets might tear into them.

Hollis waded into the field, firing bursts from his Bren and calling out to the two concealed soldiers. Under his covering fire, the men jumped to their feet and ran towards the safety of the farmhouse wall. Hollis backed away, still shooting, as the Germans realized what was happening. He had to zigzag to make himself a difficult target, with bullets zinging around him, tearing off great clumps of rhubarb and thudding into the soil at his feet.

But Hollis didn't turn and run until he was sure the other men were out of danger. Only when he saw them find cover did he think of saving himself. He reached the farmhouse after a hair-raising dash across the field - filthy, breathless, but unhurt.

Stanley Hollis had done it again.

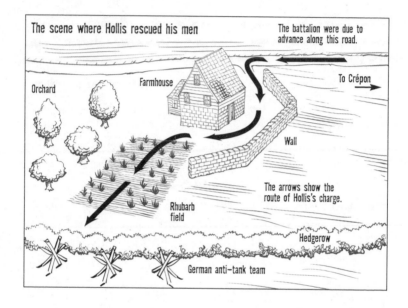

The scene where Hollis rescued his men

The battalion were due to advance along this road.

To Crépon

Orchard

Farmhouse

Wall

The arrows show the route of Hollis's charge.

Rhubarb field

Hedgerow

German anti-tank team

The British army has estimated that the odds of surviving a VC-winning action are no more than one in ten, which goes to explain why the majority of the medals are awarded posthumously. But, in the long history of the VC, only three men have won the medal twice. They received a bar, to be worn across the top of the cross. Army rules state that the medal-winning actions must take place on different dates. So, although Hollis performed two VC-winning acts, he didn't qualify for a bar. But he wasn't bitter. One VC is enough for any soldier.

In September 1944, Hollis was badly injured by a

German mortar shell. His fighting days were finally over. He was recovering in a hospital back home in England when the news came that he'd won the medal. In the following years, he settled down to his job as a landlord, never complaining to his family or friends about the terrible pain he suffered because of his combat injuries.

He died in February 1972, at the age of 51. His VC is on display at the Green Howards Regimental Museum, Richmond, North Yorkshire.

It is one of the museum's most prized possessions.

The cliff climbers

In May 1942, U.S. army chiefs decided to create a battalion of elite, special forces, capable of raiding deep into enemy territory. Unlike the *Wehrmacht*, who structured their divisions in a strict hierarchy according to the quality of soldiers and their equipment, U.S. troops aimed for a common standard of proficiency. On the whole, this was an advantage, as every division had to be battle-ready and carefully trained. But some missions called for units of specialist soldiers, tutored in the arts of camouflage, self-sufficiency and silent killing.

As a model for their new battalion, the American generals looked to the British commandos, small units of soldiers who were experts in amphibious attacks and close combat techniques. The commando - from the South African Boer word *kommando*, a light, attacking cavalry group - was a brainchild of Winston Churchill's. After the retreat from Europe in 1940, the British Prime Minister refused to accept a passive, defensive role for his country's armed forces. He wanted to show the Germans - and his own people - that Britain was still in the war. Large-scale raids were too risky, but a platoon of commandos could strike anywhere along the German-held coasts, causing mayhem before slipping back to their boats.

They were a guerrilla force, following Churchill's orders to 'butcher and bolt' and disregarding conventional military tactics. After raids in Norway, Italy, the Channel Islands and the Middle East, they were so dreaded by coastal defenders, Hitler was prompted to give his infamous *Kommandobefehl* - commando order - in October 1942. Incensed by the near mythic status of these special forces, he instructed his troops to execute all captured commandos, even if they were injured or attempting to surrender. This was in breach of the 1929 Geneva Convention on military conduct, and several prominent Nazis would later hang for it as a war crime.

Commandos were recruited from every sector of the armed forces - even the civilian police - in a quest for the best possible candidates. They trained at a remote castle in the highlands of Scotland, mastering boatcraft, cliff climbing, special weapons and orienteering. A commando was expected to run ten miles in 90 minutes and during exercises he was constantly shelled with live ammunition. Only a few of the applicants made it through the course.

It was June 1942 when the first volunteers for the American special forces arrived at the Scottish camp. They took everything their commando tutors could throw at them and passed the course with distinction. The U.S. Rangers were up and running.

Their name was chosen as a tribute to the 'backwoodsmen' and pioneers of the early American frontier, men who had scouted and 'ranged' across forests and plains when the country was a virgin wilderness. The term had later been adopted as an expression for resourceful, expert soldiers or marshals, who roamed from Texas to California.

Thousands of U.S. servicemen applied to join the Ranger battalions - but only a few hundred were selected. In March 1943, 2nd Ranger Battalion was formed at Camp Forrest, Tennessee. The exercise regime was even tougher than it had been in Scotland. In particular, Rangers were trained to keep advancing under heavy enemy fire. The volunteers must have asked themselves if there was a good reason for their brutal workload. What did the army need Rangers for, anyway?

On June 6, 1944, they got their answer. Three companies - around 250 men - from 2nd Ranger Battalion were ordered to storm and destroy the clifftop gun emplacements at Pointe du Hoc, France. "The most dangerous mission of D-Day," was how General Omar Bradley, one of the most senior *Overlord* commanders, described it.

Pointe du Hoc was a spur of sheer cliffs, 100 feet high, jutting out from the Norman coast. The Germans had positioned six 155mm guns on its heights, and surrounded them with mines, barbed wire, machine-gun nests and a network of hidden trenches - all facing the land approach to the battery. They weren't expecting any attack from the sea. Who would be crazy enough to attempt one?

An infantry garrison of some 200 men from the 726th Infantry Regiment was dug in across this lonely place. For months, they'd endured Allied bombing raids, until the surface of their 30-acre enclosure was pockmarked and scarred with craters. They had little to do but work on strengthening the position and check their guns. Each artillery piece had a range of ten miles, and could bombard ships at sea or pound long stretches of the sandy beaches curling to the east and west: *Utah* and *Omaha*. The Germans didn't know it, but their guns were situated right in the middle of the planned invasion. Somebody was going to have to take the Pointe away from them.

The commander of 2nd Battalion, Lt. Colonel James Earl Rudder - or 'Big Jim' - was the man chosen for the job. Rudder was a 34-year-old, no-nonsense Texan, who had been educated at a military college and was active in the U.S. Army reserves before war broke out. He'd worked as a teacher and college football coach and knew how to get the best out of his men. Although Rudder believed Rangers were the finest soldiers alive, he was under no illusions about the dangers of his mission. After scaling the cliffs and overrunning the gun emplacements, he was expected to advance nearly a mile inland to an asphalt coast road and set up a defensive perimeter against German counterattacks. There would be nowhere to run to if his lines were broken and, since Rangers were classed as commandos by the Nazis, surrender was not an option. His men would fight to the death.

Rudder planned a surprise LCA assault for 06:30, splitting his force to ascend both sides of the Pointe simultaneously. He called this group Task Force A.

Task Force B was made up of another company from 2nd Ranger Battalion and the bulk of 5th Battalion. Their job was to wait off the cliffs in a cluster of circling LCAs, until Rudder sent a signal to say his men had taken the Pointe. Task Force B would then land as reinforcements. If there was no signal by 07:00, they should assume the attack had failed and make for *Omaha Beach*, to rendezvous with another company from 2nd Battalion. From there, the Rangers could rush across country to reach the Pointe and destroy the guns.

Rudder was a pragmatist. He realized that any plan is nothing more than a few words of intent, and there were a dozen things that could go wrong with his. But he knew from his coaching days that the outcome of any contest usually comes down to the stamina and quality of the players. He put all his faith in his men.

At 04:05, from 19 km (12 miles) out at sea, the Pointe was savaged with high explosives from American bombers and the huge guns of *USS Texas*, *USS Satterlee* and *HMS Talybont*. The Rangers' target was suddenly illuminated by the shelling, a flaming beacon on the horizon. At 04:30 they started the long journey to the shore, packed inside 9 LCAs, accompanied by two LCA supply craft and three amphibious DUKW trucks - known as *ducks*. The ducks had been fitted with 100-foot extending ladders, on loan from the London Fire Brigade. Each LCA carried six rocket-propelled grappling hooks fitted to heavy cables or rope ladders. The Rangers themselves packed sections of lightweight steel ladders that could be snapped together. They were also equipped with hand-held rockets and lines. Rudder was willing to try anything to get up those cliffs.

Within minutes of setting out, one of the LCA supply boats rolled over on a big wave and sank - five men were drowned. Another LCA wallowed on the waves before turning over, spilling men into the freezing water. Most of the crew was rescued by a ship where doctors treated them for hypothermia. They were evacuated to England, despite their pleas to rejoin the battalion.

Rudder cursed the sinkings, but he had more immediate concerns. Shielding his eyes against the saltwater spray, he studied the landmarks along the coast. His lead LCA was off course, moving away from the Pointe.

"What's going on?" he cried to the boatswain. "We're heading for *Omaha Beach*."

"Must be the current, sir," the man at the wheel explained. "We were warned it might be strong flowing to the east."

"Then aim to the west," Rudder snapped.

The LCA turned into the waves, correcting its course. Rudder had lost precious minutes and now his fleet of Rangers was 'broadside-on' to the defenders. One sergeant heard a crack next to his head. When he turned around there was a hole in the side of his craft big enough for a golf ball to pass through. The Germans were targeting the Rangers with cannon and artillery fire. Rangers took what cover they could on the slippery floors of their LCAs.

At 07:00, Task Force A was at last closing on Pointe du Hoc. Rudder decided to cancel the attack on the west cliffs, as he was running out of time. So all 9 boats made for a pebbly beach on the eastern side. The German defenders were by now recovering from the aerial and fleet bombardment and they strafed the approaching craft with their Spandau machine guns. One of the ducks took a direct hit from a shell and broke apart in the water. It wasn't until 07:08 that Rudder's LCAs crunched onto the bank of pebbles and the men spilled out. The delay in landing had lost them their reinforcements. Task Force B had left for *Omaha* - and with them any hope of surprising the defenders.

As they struggled ashore - drenched, heavy-legged and seasick - at least 20 Rangers were cut down by bullets, or torn apart by German 'potato-masher' grenades (so called because of their stick and drumhead design) tossed from the cliff ramparts. Some Rangers had to swim the last few yards carrying all their kit. Others were swallowed by underwater craters made by naval shells that had fallen short of their target. These shell holes were up to 30 feet wide and the men had to skirt them in their rush up the beach. Bodies floated in these treacherous ponds. It was a scene of carnage, but the Rangers didn't pause for a second. As soon as they reached the base of the cliffs, they set to work.

Although most of the soldiers were only lightly armed, some carried 20-round BARs - Browning Automatic Rifles - which were as powerful as Bren guns. And each LCA had a Lewis machine gun too. Rudder ordered his gunners to rake the clifftops with bullets, driving the defenders away from the edge.

As they settled on the beach, the LCAs fired their grappling rockets. In a huge ball of sparks and smoke, the projectile dragged a line up to the plateau above the cliffs. As it fell back, the steel teeth of the grapple dug into the earth. To stop the Germans from rushing over and dislodging the grapple teeth, the Americans had fixed imitation fuses to them, which hissed and fizzed like a lit stick of dynamite. But not all of the defenders were fooled. As the Rangers scrambled up the ropes, some of them crashed back to earth gripping a cut line. The bulk of the grappling lines were waterlogged and this extra weight reduced their efficiency. But the hand-held lines fared a little better, and soon there was a web of ropes strung all over the face of the cliff.

While the Rangers struggled up wet and muddy ropes, digging their daggers into the rocks for a solid grip, the duck crews were still trying to land. Unlike the flat-bottomed LCAs, they couldn't get past the bomb craters in the shingle, so their extending ladders were too far from the cliff wall to be of much use. This didn't stop some of the Rangers from raising the ladders and firing the Lewis guns fixed at their top. Sergeant William Stivison was reeled 80 feet into the air on a ladder, where he swayed from side to side on his duck's rhythm across the waves. As he rocked like a human pendulum, Stivison blasted at the defenders and taunted them across the void. The Germans tried to knock him off his perch with machine gun and small-arms fire - but to no avail. Stivison survived his antics on the swinging ladder.

For two years the Rangers had been training hard, in all weathers and in all terrains, and always under fire. Nothing was going to stop them from getting up that cliff. It started with one man making it to the top, then crouching down to help the soldier behind him. Soon, groups of two or three Rangers had scrambled up and were returning fire on the Germans. Each man who finished the climb made it easier for the next to succeed. A few minutes after arriving on the beach, there were small squads of Rangers running inland, pushing forward against snipers, machine-gun nests and mortar explosions. By 07:45, Rudder was able to send a coded radio signal - *Praise the Lord* - to the warships prowling in the Channel. His force had beaten the cliffs. The Rangers were on Pointe Du Hoc, and fighting for their lives.

Rudder set up his command post in a bomb crater next to a smashed concrete bunker, while his men rushed out across the torn landscape of the Pointe. The German troops had retreated to their underground bunkers, only popping their heads above ground to let off a few shots before disappearing again. It was hard to keep track of the enemy in this shell-blasted plateau. In every crater there was the risk of a grenade attack, a sniper's bullet or a bayonet in the back. But the Rangers kept closing on the emplacements and finally stormed their way in.

The guns were gone. All that remained were telegraph pole dummies resting on the artillery blocks, left there to confuse aerial reconnaissance. Some of the gun positions weren't even fortified and lacked a roof. Rudder guessed that the Germans had moved their guns to a safe location inland until the bunkers were completed.

It was a blow for the colonel. At least 20 of his men had died on the beach and the rest were trapped on the plateau. But, instead of hesitating or reflecting on his situation, he ordered his troops to proceed with the next stage of the mission: to secure the coast road. Gradually infiltrating the labyrinth of tunnels and trenches scraped out of the Pointe, the Rangers advanced due south, fighting for every yard.

Back at the command post, Rudder tried to secure the seaward regions of the Pointe. The battle for territory was by no means over, as the Germans still manned an anti-aircraft gun on the western side of the cliffs and a machine-gun nest on the eastern side. The command post was itself under fire, and Rudder had already been shot in the leg by a sniper. He strode around the mud trenches defiantly, snarling orders and driving his men on.

From the beginning of the raid, *USS Satterlee* had been assisting the Rangers with carefully aimed salvos. Radio reception was crackly and unreliable, but two navy fire-control spotters attached to the Rangers had been helping the ship target to German positions. Rudder asked them to fix the coordinates for the machine gun nest and request the battleship to destroy it. But, with only a second's screech as a warning, a stray 'marker' shell from another warship landed bang on the command post, damaging the radio and killing both spotters. Rudder was wounded in the right arm, and parts of his body were painted yellow from the marker liquid.

Dragging himself onto his feet, the colonel quickly recovered. He ordered his radioman, Lieutenant Wilmot Eikner, to send the message. It was now impossible to reach the ship by radio, so Eikner set up an antique signal lamp he'd had the foresight to bring along in the supply boat. He had also packed some carrier pigeons and planned to send written messages, strapped to their legs. He alerted the ship using an adaptation of Morse code, with long and short flashes. The ship's captain brought her guns close in to shore, and gouged out a great chunk of cliff that had been the foundation for the machine-gun pillbox. Rudder and his men watched it tumble into the sea, and cheered.

Just before 08:00, around 50 Rangers fought their way to the coast road and set up some makeshift roadblocks. It wasn't really a case of defending the Pointe against enemy counterattacks, as large numbers of the enemy were still trapped inside the area. But, the Rangers hoped to mop-up the remaining Germans in the course of the morning. In the meantime, they needed a boundary line, and they had grenades, their BARs and one bazooka to enforce it.

Sergeants Len Lomell and Jack Kuhn were patrolling the fields along the coast road when they came across a rough track with some peculiar markings in the ground. Rangers were trained to be inquisitive, so the two men nodded at each other and began scouting along the track. After moving almost a mile inland, they stopped at a grassy dip. Lomell noticed there was something camouflaged on the other side of the hedgerow. Peering over, he saw five of the Pointe du Hoc guns, neatly arranged, with their ammunition piled next to them.

"It's them," he hissed to his friend. "One's missing. We must have got it in the air-raid."

"Where're the guards?" whispered Kuhn, fearing a trap.

But Lomell had spotted a large group of Germans a few hundred yards away, gathered around an officer giving a speech.

"Hand me your thermite grenades," whispered Lomell.

"I've only got two. But here they are."

Armed with the grenades, Lomell flipped himself over the hedge and crawled stealthily to the guns. He primed the grenades and fixed them to the traversing mechanisms of two of the guns. Thermite grenades contained chemicals hot enough to melt steel once they were exposed to the air, so the guns were welded into one position, rendering them useless. Next, he smashed all five gun sights so the weapons couldn't be aimed accurately. When he got back to where Kuhn was hiding, the two men raced back to their friends at the coast road to collect more grenades, before returning to finish the job.

It was 08:30 and the Rangers had fulfilled their primary mission; they had taken Pointe du Hoc and disabled the guns.

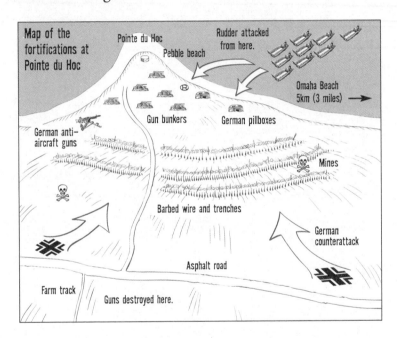

Map of the fortifications at Pointe du Hoc

Pointe du Hoc

Pebble beach

Rudder attacked from here.

Omaha Beach 5km (3 miles) →

Gun bunkers

German pillboxes

German anti-aircraft guns

Mines

Barbed wire and trenches

German counterattack

Asphalt road

Farm track

Guns destroyed here.

Rudder didn't hear the news until 09:00. The usually stony-faced colonel permitted himself a rare smile, then got back to the business at hand. The Rangers still had to hold the Pointe. For two nights and a day they fought off a series of ferocious German counterattacks, until only 90 men from the 225 raiders were still standing. Forces led by Brigadier

The cliff climbers

General Cota - the man who gave the famous command, "Rangers, lead the way," on *Omaha Beach* - arrived on the morning of June 8. Surveying the battle-scarred acres of the plateau, Cota commended the Rangers on their heroism. Rudder and five other Pointe du Hoc veterans were awarded the DSC - the Distinguished Service Cross. After the war, the French government dedicated the Pointe as a memorial site to the Americans. A white granite pylon looms over the remains of a bunker, carved into the shape of a Ranger's dagger.

Ten years after the raid, Rudder returned to Pointe du Hoc and the memorial with his young son. During the visit he stared long and hard at the towering cliffs, then turned to the reporter accompanying him and asked: "Will someone please tell me how we did this?"

Shermans in the surf

The young tank officer bit his lip and tried to concentrate on staying awake. He must have fallen asleep during the briefing. The weeks of relentless combat training on the Welsh mountains had taken their toll and he was exhausted. Even now, he found it hard to shake off the dream he'd been having. Before him was the open sea, foaming with great waves, black and wild under a blood-red sky. The sight of the ocean made him shudder. At least he was safe, sheltered inside the turret of his tank, a brand-new Sherman M4. There were other tanks behind him, all resting in the belly of a huge ship. He reassured himself that he must be on some kind of transport vessel, carrying his tank troop to a friendly port. But, as he watched in horror, the bow of the ship started to tilt forward. Like a steel drawbridge crashing down, it slammed into the waves. The sea rushed in, licking at the tracks of his tank. Before he could cry out that the ship was sinking, he heard an engine rumbling into life. The next instant, his Sherman was creeping forward, picking up speed as it powered towards the engulfing ocean.

"What a nightmare," the officer chuckled, nodding to the man sitting next to him. "For a second there I was dreaming of going for a swim in a Sherman."

The other man raised an eyebrow. "Haven't you been listening, mate?" he replied sharply. "That's exactly what they're expecting us to do."

Shermans in the surf

The Allied generals who sat down to plan the invasion of occupied Europe had an expert understanding of military history. Many of them had served in the First World War and were only too aware of the tactical similarities between the fortified Normandy beaches and the unassailable trenches of the Western front, the scene of so much slaughter in that earlier conflict. The lessons of trench warfare had forced the army to revise their tactics. Even when supported by heavy artillery fire, waves of advancing infantry could be annihilated by dug-in troops armed with machine guns. The Allies had total control of the sky, but to crack the Atlantic Wall their soldiers needed an extra advantage. D-Day strategists wondered if it might be possible to land tanks just before the infantry arrived, to provide protection as well as shocking the defenders into submission.

The American Navy already had huge Landing Craft Tank boats which could ferry five or six Sherman tanks to the beaches. But these boats made attractive targets for German gunners while still miles out at sea. And, because of their size, were vulnerable to floating mines and underwater obstacles in shallow water. They also robbed the tank crews of one of their greatest advantages in battle: the element of surprise. But, without an LCT, how could a tank reach the shore?

Casting around for a solution, the planners soon heard whispers about a Hungarian engineer who had a reputation for inventing bizarre vehicles. He was working on a new design: a swimming tank.

Shermans in the surf

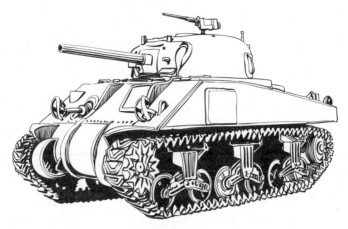

A Sherman tank

Nicholas Straussler was a middle-aged refugee from Nazi Germany, who had been toying with the idea of an amphibious tank since the 1920s. After building a series of failed prototypes using bolt-on floats, he hit on the idea of fixing a canvas screen to a temporary 'deck' welded around the top of a tank's tracks, creating an artificial hull. The tank would be hidden from sight behind this hull, which looked a little like an enormous baby buggy. Using compressed air, the tank crew could inflate the screen just before entering the sea, then discard it as soon as they reached dry land. The Shermans would suddenly appear on the beaches with their guns blazing.

For propulsion, Straussler invented a two-propeller rack that ran off the tank drive system. This 'Duplex Drive' gave the tanks their nickname - *DDs*. First tests on DDs showed that on a glass-smooth sea they could manage around 8km (5 miles) an hour. Straussler was hailed as a design genius. His canvas screen and propellers could be fitted to most tanks in only a few hours. They offered the strategists everything they'd wanted: simplicity, ruggedness and surprise. Over 2,000 tanks were converted into DDs during the run-up to the invasion.

But not everyone was happy with these amphibious monsters. Their crews reacted to the plan with a mixture of terror and disbelief.

Lieutenant Stuart Hills was a young tank commander from the Sherwood Rangers, who'd been sent off on a training course to learn about DDs. Hills had never liked the sea, and the thought of taking a tank out for a swim struck him as odd, to say the least. But he tried to be positive about his assignment. He realized the beach landings were essential to bring the war to an end, and he wanted to see the Axis powers smashed as quickly as possible. He had personal reasons for craving a rapid Allied victory.

Hills was a 19-year-old novice, fresh from the British Army military academy at Sandhurst. But he was tough and independent, and already knew how to handle himself in an institutional environment like the army. He was a veteran of one of the hardest training camps ever devised: the English public school system. Hills' parents lived in the British colony of Hong Kong and, like many expatriates, they wanted their children to be educated in Britain. At the age of seven, Hills was put in boarding school, making only occasional trips home. During his teens he was at

Tonbridge School, where he excelled at cricket, boxing and rugby. These sports became a passion for him, and he paid little attention to all the talk about politics and the likelihood of war. But events in Europe couldn't be ignored. Early in 1939, Hills waved good-bye to his father, who'd come along to watch him play rugby before sailing for the Orient.

By 1940, the schoolboy was lying on his back in a Kent field, gazing up at dogfights between Spitfires and Messerschmitts. When Hong Kong fell to the Japanese in December 1941, Hill's mother and father were reported missing. The family villa had been shelled until it was reduced to rubble and local residents were either shot or interned in brutal prison camps. Alone in England, Hills had no way of knowing if his parents were dead or alive. His best chance of seeing them again would be a speedy conclusion to the war. In July 1942, he enlisted in the army and by the age of 20 he was commanding a troop of three tanks.

The Sherwood Rangers began their DD training in a small British Valentine tank, floating in the middle of a freezing cold lake in Essex. The tank commander stood on a wooden shelf fixed behind the turret. This allowed him to peer over the canvas screen, while the other men sat in their positions in the body of the tank, six feet below the water line. They were given the same emergency breathing equipment used by submariners, which did nothing for their nerves. Even in perfect conditions, water poured over the screen once the tank got underway. A bilge pump for clearing leaks and traditional army 'stiff-upper-lip' kept them going, but the men couldn't help wondering what the ride would be like on the open sea.

The first ocean-going tests in a DD Sherman were off the Isle of Wight, when Hills launched his tank from the ramp of an LCT. Although the Sherman weighed around twice as much as a Valentine, to Hills' delight it didn't immediately sink below the waves. In calm seas, the crew managed runs of up to 5km (3 miles) into shore. There were still complaints from some of the men, annoyed when their request for danger money from the naval authorities was ignored. The daily rum ration - a navy perk - made up for some of their grievances.

Although the crews could see the lighter side of their DD antics, they knew the risks they were taking. At least seven tanks sank on training runs, off Poole in Dorset. Other sinkings were hushed up as part of the D-Day security measures. Wrecked DD Valentines have become dive sites in recent years. Some of them are war graves - the bodies of the crew were never retrieved from their steel cells.

The Normandy invasion was unprecedented in scale and ambition. For any chance of success it relied on technological innovation combined with human daring. Transporting hundreds of thousands of soldiers, their equipment - even their tanks - tested the Allies to their limits. Hills and his men may not have liked their new role as Sherman boatmen, but their impatience to get into the fighting was greater than any doubts they had about the swimming tanks. The men might have grumbled, but they accepted the dangers of the mission.

They loaded up on the night of June 4, 1944 and passed the next day anchored off their own coastline. The weather was so filthy, even the sailors among them were seasick. But Eisenhower couldn't afford to recall the ships to port; it would have risked the secrecy and momentum of the invasion. His attacking force had no option but to sit it out, waiting for the signal to depart. Hills' men huddled under a canvas sheet they'd draped between the tanks on the LCT, trying forlornly to keep themselves dry and cheerful despite the gales. Everything around them was wet and slimy, sticky with spilled diesel fuel, food scraps and vomit. Even the rum ration was hard to keep down.

In the afternoon the fleet gathered up all its stragglers and storm-tossed drifters, massing them in a 5000-ship flotilla and turning every bow to the east. *Operation Neptune* - the Allied naval assault - had begun. The ships filed into ten 'sea lanes' that had been cleared of German mines, slowly forming stepping-stone bridges of steel, spanning out into the Channel. It took over 250 minesweepers to clear these lanes. The armada pouring into them was truly an Allied effort, with ships from Britain, America, France, Canada, Poland, Greece, Holland and Norway taking part. In Normandy, the defenders asleep in their concrete dens had no suspicion of the threat approaching over the horizon. Their weather stations reported foul conditions and so the officers on watch assumed there was no possibility of enemy naval activity. Besides, the tides were all wrong for an invasion attempt. Why should they be worried, when their own chief commander, Field Marshal Rommel, was so relaxed he was on leave in Germany celebrating his wife's 50th birthday?

At midnight, Hills heard the bass note hum of British Halifax bombers crossing the night sky. They were towing the gliders carrying the *Pegasus* bridge raiders, one of whom, Lieutenant Sandy Smith, had been in the year above Hills at Tonbridge.

At the stern of the LCT there was a dim cabin where the officers gathered and ripped open their sealed orders. They had been studying maps and factsheets relating to beaches for months, but this was the first time they were given the exact location and objective of their mission. Hills and his troop of three Shermans were to land on the western end of *Gold Beach*, emerging from the surf at H-Hour minus five minutes. They had to destroy the pillboxes and gun emplacements that might threaten the infantry cresting over the waves behind them.

Hills was too brave and too confident to panic about his chances of making it off the beach. Unlike the veteran crew in his tank, who'd all served in North Africa and seen the frailty of men in the 'steel storm' of combat, Hills couldn't imagine himself dying in the next few hours. Like many soldiers before their first battle, he still felt indestructible.

He decided he wouldn't bother with a lifejacket when it was time to launch.

At 04:30, the dawn light gave the crews their first view of the invasion panorama. The sea was crowded with ships, from great battleships to fragile landing craft. When the naval barrage started just before six, Hills saw the coast erupt in fire. The oranges and reds of the explosions stood out brilliantly against a grey sea and overcast sky.

With the launch approaching, Hills and his crew took up their positions in their tank. Two men settled down in the Sherman's belly: the driver and machine gunner. Above them perched the main gunner and radioman. Hills clambered onto the wooden platform at the rear of the turret and gave the order to inflate the canvas screen. He was the only man in the Sherman who would have a view of the battlefield, peering over the canopy and shielding his eyes against the freezing spray.

The launch was supposed to begin almost four miles from the beach, but Hills' squadron leader thought the sea looked too rough for his DDs. If they had to struggle against strong currents and waves, they might be late landing on the beach and the infantry would be left unprotected. He decided to take the LCTs closer in, to a few hundred yards from the shore.

The news met with a mixed reaction from the tank crews. They were glad to be reducing the distance of their ocean ride. But soon they would be within close range of the German artillery and heavy machine guns. Watching his LCT ramp lower into the sea, Hills noticed the impact of shells and the splash and patter of bullets slicing around the ship. The enemy was already getting their range.

But it was time to go. Orders screeched through his radio headset and the tank's diesel engine coughed into life. Hills gave the order to advance onto the ramp, but his driver halted as a sailor darted across their path, waving his arms. There was a fault with the mechanism holding the ramp in place. Hills would have to delay the launch for a few seconds, long enough to glance at the beach pitching before him. Two British Churchill tanks were outlined against the dunes, both billowing flames. Hills could see they'd been ripped apart by artillery shells and the survivors machine-gunned as they jumped to the sand.

The sight reminded Hills of stories he'd heard from the North Africa veterans, about tanks catching fire - or 'brewing up' - was one of a tanker's greatest fears. Shermans were infamous for their tendency to burst into flames at the first hit. The Germans called them *Tommy-cookers* (after *Tommy*, the nickname for a British soldier). Allied tankers named them *Ronson-lighters*, after a popular brand of cigarette lighter that was guaranteed to light first time. The ramp was ready. A shell exploded just to the side of the LCT. Another tore into the ship's hull. Men were screaming.

"Go, go, go," Hills ordered, and the tank lurched forward, rolled down the ramp and slid into the waves. This enormously heavy steel vehicle weighed down on the canvas screen and Hills watched it wobble and stretch at every seam. But they were floating. The DD was carrying them towards the beach.

But soon the driver's voice was hissing in Hills' headset: "We're taking water." It was already lapping around his knees.

Hills calmly instructed his crew to start pumping the water out, but still the water kept rising. When the commander saw it bubbling out of the driver's hatch, he knew his tank was lost. There must have been some rupture or tear in the steel bottom of the Sherman - perhaps some shrapnel from one of the shell bursts had caught them when they were exposed on the ramp. He gave the order to abandon the tank.

The men only had seconds to squeeze out of their hatches. Shells and bullets were still whipping around them as the gunner inflated a small rubber dinghy. Hills rolled into it from the turret, and the others joined him as it scraped over the canvas screen and floated away. They were all watching as the tank spluttered, coughed and sank straight to the bottom.

Out of Hills' troop of three tanks, only one made it to shore - and its commander was so badly wounded by shrapnel he had to be evacuated immediately. Up and down the coast, the DDs were struggling against enemy fire and high water. On *Utah*, every one of the 28 tanks launched arrived safely on the beach. Of the 34 DDs sent into *Sword*, 11 sank or were blown up. Most of the DDs bound for *Juno* got through. But

Omaha, unlucky in so many respects that morning, saw terrible tank losses. That beach was more exposed to the rage of the Atlantic than the other landing sites, and tanks simply rolled out onto the pounding waves and vanished under the waves. One battalion lost 29 of their swimming Shermans. Out of the DD force approaching Hills' target, *Gold* Beach, 13 tanks went to the bottom.

Hundreds of tankers died that morning, trying to get to shore. But the majority of the DDs got through, and their contribution to the infantry attack saved the lives of thousands.

Hills only had a few moments to reflect on the loss of his Sherman before turning his mind to more pressing matters. He and his crew had lost all their kit inside the sinking tank. They were cold and exhausted, had no food, maps or weapons, and were bobbing around without oars in the middle of a battle zone. The bright yellow dinghy could hardly have been more conspicuous: it was practically an invitation for some target practice. As they drifted with the offshore currents, a shell plopped into the sea just ahead of them and exploded. It didn't do any damage, but when Hills saw a second shell slam into the water behind them, he quickly realized what was happening. A German gunner was 'zeroing in' on them, using the first two shots to plot his aim. The third shell would land right among them, vaporizing the dinghy and all the occupants.

But the tankers were finally due a stroke of luck. A

fast Landing Craft Gun boat - an LCG - powered up alongside the dinghy and hurried the men on board. As it surged away, the third shell exploded in the water, but its prey had already slipped the hook.

Hills and his men sipped whisky and ate Mars bars below decks, trying to regain their strength. In the afternoon they watched the battle unfold from the deck of the patrol craft, wondering how the Sherwood Rangers were faring against the Germans. It wasn't until D-Day plus 1 that the LCG captain found them another dinghy and sent them off to shore. They splashed out of the surf looking like a party of shipwrecked mariners, bedraggled, bagless and dazed. There was a long walk ahead of them, to rejoin the regiment, but Hills and his men had arrived on *Gold Beach*. They were now part of the Normandy invasion.

Lieutenant Stuart Hills had a lot of hard fighting ahead of him. He took command of a new Sherman and battled his way across France, then deep into Germany, winning a Military Cross for his bravery.

In 1946 he was finally reunited with his parents. They had endured more than three years of hardship in Japanese camps. Without the courage and stamina of men like their son, their internment could have lasted much longer.

The dice are on the carpet...

There was a fire that night in the small market town of Ste. Mère-Eglise. A house on the main square was roaring and hissing with flames. 20-year-old Raymond Paris heard the church bells ringing, the commotion in the streets and the cries for help. He joined his father, a volunteer fireman, and ran over to where some water pumps and hoses were stored. With the help of another man they began dragging the heavy equipment towards the square, where a chain of people were passing buckets to a group of firefighters. German soldiers mingled with the gaping crowd, or lingered at the edge of the square. They had lifted their nightly curfew so the townspeople could tackle the blaze. For three years, Ste. Mère-Eglise had been a ghost town between sunset and sunrise. The sight of so many people rushing about in the darkness made the German patrols nervous.

Raymond was sweating and out of breath when he reached the square. He stretched his arms to straighten his back and glanced up at the sky. Coming out of the west, hundreds of planes speckled the heavens. They were so close to the ground he could make out their markings - it was the US Army Air Force.

"Not another bombing raid," grumbled his father. "That's all we need."

But the planes droned by and vanished into the night, and father and son went back to their work. They had joined the chain and were filling buckets from a hand *pump when the second wave of planes appeared.*

This time, the Germans lifted their Schmeisser machine guns in panic and started blasting at the squadrons passing overhead. They were used to bombing raids, but these planes were flying much lower than usual - and there were so many of them. The townspeople concentrated on the house fire.

When the third wave of aircraft came a few minutes later, Raymond saw thousands of men tumbling out of them, fluttering towards the town like huge snowflakes with their rippling silk parachutes. "It's the invasion," he shouted, waving his arms to welcome the Americans. "They're coming."

A German knocked him to one side and started shooting, trying to hold back a blizzard of paratroopers from falling across the town...

Around 13,000 American paratroopers from two airborne divisions dropped into France in the early hours of June 6, 1944. Most of these men landed to the west of *Utah Beach*, in a wide band stretching across the Cotentin peninsula, the western tip of Normandy. Their main task was to protect the American beachheads and isolate the German garrison at the port of Cherbourg.

The Allies had constructed two *Mulberries* - huge concrete docking stations - to receive troops and supplies in the first weeks of the invasion. But it takes a huge number of cargo ships to supply and feed an invading army, so they wanted to capture a major Channel port as soon as possible. Cherbourg was heavily defended against any assault from the sea, but more vulnerable to a land attack. Paratroopers from the 82nd All American Airborne Division - so called because its soldiers came from every state in the country - were ordered to cut the railway, road and communication links to the port's German garrison, in preparation for the infantry arriving through *Utah*. One of the largest of the paratroopers' six 'drop-zones', named DZ-O, was the area around Ste. Mère-Eglise (population around 2,000) lying on the main road between Cherbourg and Caen.

The first units to jump into Normandy were 20 'pathfinder' teams who had the job of marking out the DZs with lamps or chunky radar devices. These machines acted like beacons for the pilots of the Dakota aircraft transporting the main attack force and helped them to time their drops accurately. The pathfinders flew over the Channel in the opening minutes of June 6.

The earliest paratrooper 'stick' - a planeload of about 16 men - hit the ground at 12:16. It was commanded by Captain Frank Lillyman from the 101st Screaming Eagles Airborne Division (named after their uniform insignia, an open-mouthed profile of the bird). This made Lillyman and his men the first American soldiers to land in France on D-Day, at exactly the same time as Major John Howard and his platoons arrived at *Pegasus* bridge. Old soldiers who fought in the *bocage* still argue about who was first into Normandy, but it seems the British and

97

Americans are happy to agree that they arrived simultaneously.

As was often the case on D-Day, the pathfinders' landings didn't go exactly to plan. Some of the men found themselves trading bullets with bewildered German patrols while they were still descending. Others landed in a deep swamp running along the eastern side of the peninsula, which the enemy had secretly flooded. Tangled up in their parachutes and weighed down with equipment, many drowned.

But the biggest problem was location: pathfinders were dropped miles away from their targets. June 6 was a misty night and the Dakota pilots couldn't see any landmarks below them to help check their course. If this wasn't alarming enough, aircrews who hadn't seen combat before were terrified by the thick wall of flak thrown up by German gun batteries. Thinking it was impassable, they flew too fast, too high or diverted from their correct flight plan to avoid it.

So the 300 pathfinders were left scattered all over the Cotentin peninsula, and they had a difficult job even to find the DZs. While they puzzled over their maps and struggled to mark out the few landing areas they could reach, 800 planes were lumbering into the night sky from English airfields. In less than an hour, thousands of paratroopers would be coming down across the *bocage*, facing the same hazards and confusion that had confronted their pathfinders before them. The air invasion had only just begun, but it was already in chaos.

But Raymond Paris was not as startled as the German troops and other citizens of Ste. Mère-Eglise when he saw the Americans jumping from their planes. Raymond was active in the French Resistance, and in the early evening of June 5 he'd heard a coded radio message that warned him the Allied invasion was imminent.

Raymond had access to a tiny crystal radio set. He always tried to listen to the BBC news - and in particular to the personal messages that came towards the end of each broadcast. Most of these were garbled, idiotic statements, designed to confuse enemy eavesdroppers, but some phrases had a special meaning. Local Resistance fighters were waiting for one crucial sentence: "Les dés sont sur le tapis," or *the dice are on the carpet*. When he heard these words hissing from his radio, Raymond couldn't believe his ears. It was the signal that the Allies were about to invade - although he had no idea where or how they would come. He was pleasantly surprised when he saw the parachutes opening above his own small town.

The broadcast marked another failure for the German intelligence services. *Gestapo* agents knew all about the radio codes - they had tortured captured Resistance members for the information - and had already alerted the *Wehrmacht* about them. But the military codebreakers were so used to false alarms and Allied trickery they ignored the intercepted BBC message. Besides, they held the Resistance movement in contempt, regarding them as a disorganized rabble.

They couldn't believe the Allies would risk notifying them of any invasion plan.

The exact role the Resistance played in liberating Occupied France is still murky and uncertain, but there is no question they made a great contribution to the Allies' tactical victory on D-Day. Their information about the coastal fortifications - gleaned from local farmers, construction workers and their own reconnaissance missions - was of enormous value. Farmers were particularly useful. There was barely an inch of Normandy that was uncultivated, and Resistance-friendly farmers knew exactly what was happening on their land. The Pointe du Hoc was one of the few places along the coast with a sealed perimeter - which is why the Allies didn't know its guns had been removed before June 6. Resistance farmers simply hadn't been able to get into the enclosure to take a look.

All across France, small groups of local fighters were active saboteurs, harassing the supply network of the *Wehrmacht*. If a trainload of essential food or tanks broke down, or was delayed en route for the western front, there was a good chance the Resistance were to blame for it. They planted explosives on railway bridges, siphoned oil from vehicle engines, and even fought pitched battles with elite SS troops. The *Gestapo* were fools to dismiss them. Hundreds of Resistance fighters were tortured and executed for daring to oppose German occupation; they risked their lives for love of their country. Patriotic soldiers always make a dangerous enemy.

The dice are on the carpet...

Raymond had helped his local Resistance cell by producing forged identity and ration cards. After *Gestapo* agents arrested one of his relatives carrying some of these fake papers, Raymond worried he might be traced. So he went into hiding. He was only in Ste. Mère-Eglise by chance on June 5, secretly visiting his family. But it was a night he would remember for the rest of his life.

The paratroopers were coming down all around the square, fumbling with their lines and harnesses, trying to steer themselves away from the enemy. One American landed on the cobbles a few yards from Raymond; he rolled to the side and was up and running for cover. Amazed, Raymond watched as another soldier crashed into the branches of some lime trees and hung there, desperately kicking his legs in an effort to free himself. A group of men from the town ran over and cut him loose. Then he mumbled something in English before backing away towards the safety of the dark.

Suddenly there was the sound of screams and the rattle of gunfire coming from every direction, while in the square the church bells rang out and the burning house roared louder than ever. Raymond stared up at the sky and saw two men drifting towards the blaze. Perhaps the heat was drawing their parachutes towards it? He watched in horror as they landed among the flames and their ammunition pouches exploded. Another billowing parachute lurched towards the church and caught on the ramparts of the steeple.

The dice are on the carpet...

The paratrooper jerked to a stop and slammed into the church stones like a broken puppet, suspended high above the square. Raymond heard a shot, turned and saw a German soldier standing next to him, blasting at an American caught in the trees. He managed to distract the German just long enough for the paratrooper to scramble out of his harness and escape. Raymond realized it was too dangerous to stay in the square. There were bullets ricochetting around him and the Germans were in a state of panic, shooting at anything that moved. He slipped out of the square and ran back to his house, his mind racing with everything he'd witnessed.

Private John Steele of the 505th Paratrooper Infantry Regiment, the PIR, hadn't expected to start the war hanging from a French bell tower. His stick of parachutists was supposed to be landing in some fields a few miles to the north. But some 505th sticks were dropped as far as 22km (14 miles) off their targets. By those standards, Steele was a near miss. He'd seen Ste. Mère-Eglise as soon as he'd tumbled out of his Dakota, and he watched the shells and tracer bullets exploding all around him. Many of his friends were dead before they reached the ground and Steele himself was already injured; he'd been shot in the foot - a real paratrooper's wound.

The house on fire must have been producing powerful gusts of air, because Steele had found it impossible to control his descent. At first, he kicked and wriggled in his harness, trying to tear himself free from the tower. Two things happened to make him stop: he looked down and realized that if his parachute ripped the fall would kill him; and then a German fired a machine-gun blast to remind him there was a battle going on at ground level. So Steele played dead, hoping his friends would come to rescue him once they'd taken the town from the Germans.

There was a vicious and bloody struggle going on in the square below. At some point he must have cried out in anger or in pain, because two German snipers hiding on the tower steps heard his voice. Steele was lucky: one of the Germans wanted to shoot the enemy paratrooper, but the other man insisted on taking him prisoner. The injured Steele was dragged inside through a gothic window arch and led away as a prisoner of war.

While the Germans and Americans fought it out in the alleyways of Ste. Mère-Eglise, other paratroopers were landing and gathering around DZ-O. Lieutenant Colonel Edward Krause assembled 180 of his men and marched on the town. He persuaded a local man to act as their guide. Using his expert knowledge of the street layout, the Americans managed to defeat the German garrison after fierce hand-to-hand fighting. Shortly after four in the morning, they finally raised the 'Stars and Stripes' in the main square: Ste. Mère-Eglise was the first French town to be liberated on D-Day.

It took the locals a while to get used to the idea of their new freedom. At dawn Raymond Paris was still slumbering at the family home when one of the town's bakers rushed in to say the streets were full of soldiers. She wasn't sure who they were, but she was certain they weren't Germans. Rather than risk getting shot at, Raymond dashed upstairs to take a look from one of the windows. He saw the soldiers waving to him, and he could smell their cigarette smoke on the air. It was light, American tobacco smoke, not the dark German stuff. Raymond went down to meet the American invaders.

The soldiers were very friendly, but because Raymond spoke no English he found it difficult to question them, despite his intense curiosity about their mission and the progress of the invasion. As more and more townspeople came out to meet their Allies, a French-speaking paratrooper from the southern states of America stepped forward and helped to interpret. Raymond was stunned when he saw his first jeep spluttering towards the square, and even more so when he discovered it had arrived in France in the belly of a glider.

Getting into the spirit of international relations, Raymond's father offered some of the men a nip of Calvados - strong liquor made from apples. The first American he approached was suspicious of the golden liquid; he asked the Frenchman to take a sip before him. When he was satisfied it was safe to drink, he sampled a mouthful and immediately sang its praises. Word spread quickly and in no time there was a line of Americans waiting to try it.

Soon, the whole town was celebrating, and the French brought out their own flags to hang in the streets. Leaving behind the cheerful throng of people drinking and singing, Raymond strolled over to the square to take a look at the remains of the house that had been on fire. He was surprised to see the bodies of several paratroopers swaying in the trees. It was a sharp reminder that the war was still raging just beyond the town's boundaries. He went back to the street party, where the Americans were warning everyone that they expected a German counterattack within the hour. The battle for Ste. Mère-Eglise was far from over and, at just after eight in the morning, the first German artillery shells started landing on the town.

Raymond and his family rushed back to their house, packed a few emergency supplies and hurried to the bomb-shelter: a trench Raymond had dug in the garden to give his parents some protection from the frequent Allied bombing raids. As the barrage intensified, the earth shook until his whole body was tingling, and the air grew thick with clouds of dust.

During a lull in the attack, Raymond ran to the house to fetch some milk for his baby brother. He was in the kitchen, measuring some milk into a bottle when a shell exploded in the street outside. The blast was so powerful it ripped all the roof tiles off his house. As soon as his ears had stopped ringing he could hear a woman's screams coming from the opposite building. Although he wanted to offer his help, he knew he had to get back to the trench. Raymond's father had lived through the First World War and had warned his son that artillery shells often fell in clusters. Fearing another shell would land in the same spot any second, Raymond sprinted back towards his garden.

He was too late. As he left the house, shells began exploding all around him. Still clutching the milk bottle, Raymond hugged the ground as the blasts tore trees out of the earth and vaporized buildings. He tried to keep moving forward, never resting in the same place for more than a few seconds. It was a wise tactic. One time he looked over his shoulder and saw a shell-hole freshly gouged out of the earth where he'd just been lying. When he finally rolled into the trench, he was shaking so violently he had to wrap his arms around his body in an effort to calm down. He couldn't get the woman's screams out of his head.

Minutes later, he realized that someone was standing at the lip of the trench, pleading with him to climb out and talk. It was the woman he'd heard; her husband had been killed by the blast and she needed someone to come along and help move his body. Raymond clambered out into the bombardment again, braving the shellfire. All across his country, other men and women were doing the same thing, going to the aid of their friends and family...

D-Day had given Raymond Paris a taste of the freedom he craved after years of enemy rule, but it also provided horrific memories that would haunt him for the rest of his days. The sensational clash of armies in Normandy sometimes obscures the suffering so many civilians experienced. It took until June 8 for Ste.

Mère-Eglise to be secured by the Allies. Until then, German infantry and American paratroopers fought a savage, street-by-street contest for control of the town. Scores of houses were destroyed by artillery or tank fire and 22 townspeople lost their lives. In all, approximately 20,000 civilians died during the battle for Normandy.

If you visit the main square of Ste. Mère-Eglise today, you might notice a white parachute and the model of an American soldier hanging from the elegant 12th century church tower. The local people placed it there as a permanent tribute to the sacrifices that John Steele - and all his comrades - made on their behalf in the early hours of D-Day. Inside the church, the townspeople commissioned an elaborate stained-glass window, featuring the dove of peace, an anti-war poem and the American paratroopers' insignia.

Steele escaped from the Germans a few days after the battle and later rejoined his unit. Apart from his injured foot he was unscathed - though it took two weeks for his hearing to return, after hanging so long next to the tolling bells. He regularly visited Ste. Mère-Eglise, and the many friends he'd made there, until his death in Kentucky in 1969.

Red sand on Omaha Beach

The first wave had been in their landing boats for almost two hours when the naval bombardment started at 05:50. They watched shells from the guns of USS Texas streak across the sky and explode, raising a black curtain of smoke along the distant coast. The men covered their ears against the din. Recoil from each salvo pushed the great battleship sideways in the sea, sending waves that almost swamped their plywood landing boats. Soldiers who could bend down used their helmets to bale out the water sloshing over their boots, but most were too tightly packed together to move. All they could do was stand there and pray they wouldn't sink before making it to Omaha Beach.

They were expecting a 'walk in' across the sands, a few skirmishes with a ramshackle force of shell-shocked defenders, then a rapid advance inland. United States Army Air Force bombers had dropped 1,300 tons of explosives on Omaha that morning and the big guns of the fleet were reducing its ruined fortifications to rubble. An armada of 64 DD tanks motored towards the beach, while dozens of other Shermans and artillery pieces joined the onslaught from floating barges. Moments before the infantry landed, 10,000 rockets showered the coast in flames. It was a devastating barrage. Army officers didn't expect any determined resistance until the following day, when the German forces inland might stage a counterattack.

Coming in, the men scanned the hills behind the beach and recognized a few landmarks from their combat maps. To their surprise, the buildings and church towers of a nearby village looked intact. As the boat ramps slammed down, the soldiers stumbled into knee-high water. There was an eerie silence; they wondered if they might walk across the sands unopposed. A shout echoed around the hills, and the Germans opened fire.

Within minutes, most of the first wave were dead...

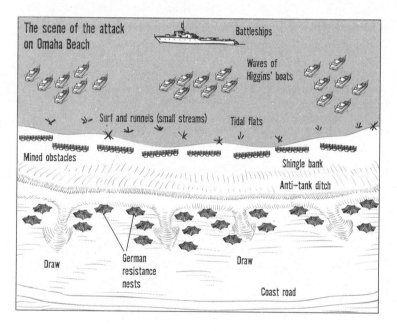

The scene of the attack on Omaha Beach

Battleships

Waves of Higgins' boats

Surf and runnels (small streams) Tidal flats

Mined obstacles Shingle bank

Anti-tank ditch

Draw German resistance nests Draw

Coast road

The French called it *La Plage d'Or* - Golden Beach - until June 6, 1944. After this date it was known as *Omaha*, adopting its *Overlord* codename, in common with the other Allied beaches. This 8km-wide (five mile) stretch of sand on the Normandy coast had been a popular tourist spot before the Second World War started, dotted with weekend cottages and a few sleepy hotels. The Germans covered it with barbed wire, minefields and bunkers. They knew that any invasion attempt on the part of the coast would have to involve capturing La Plage d'Or first. The beaches to the east - *Sword*, *Juno* and *Gold* - didn't give the Allies enough of a toehold to land their army. The beach to the west, *Utah*, was almost 40km (25miles) away from *Gold*, separated by cliffs and rocky coves. *Omaha* lay between the two flanks of the proposed landings and the Allies needed it to avoid any gaps appearing in their coastal attack.

It was an almost perfect defensive position, surrounded by steep cliffs to the east and west, and low hills, known as bluffs, a few hundred yards inland. There were only four openings suitable for vehicles in these bluffs. The Americans called them *draws*. Each draw was guarded by anti-tank guns, machine-gun nests and minefields, all connected by an intricate network of trenches. The beach itself was strewn with obstacles. But, because of tidal erosion in the area, it couldn't be mined.

The Germans used all their ingenuity to get around this problem, fixing their mines to tree-trunks, driven into the sand. At the top of the beach there was a high bank of shingle, or pebbles, which they covered with barbed wire. To get past this and reach the bluffs, a soldier had to cross a swamp and anti-tank ditch, all mined and wired. The shingle bank looked like a good place to take cover. But, like so many things about

Omaha, it was not what it seemed. The Germans had repeatedly fired their mortars and artillery, testing the range, so their shells fell along the sheltered side of the bank. Every inch of the beach was covered. There was simply nowhere to hide.

The Allies knew the *Omaha* attack was risky. On August 19, 1942, they'd tried to seize the heavily-defended port of Dieppe in *Operation Jubilee.* The surprise amphibious attack by Canadian troops, joined by two British commando units and 50 US Rangers, was a disaster from the start. Of the 5,000 men who made it to shore, 60% were killed, wounded or captured. In the battle for control of the sky, the *Luftwaffe* shot down 119 Allied planes.

But a lot had changed since the Dieppe raid. The *Luftwaffe* was all but destroyed and Allied intelligence suggested that the 800 defenders at *Omaha* came from the 716th Infantry Division: a few old men and dejected Russian former prisoners of war. They calculated that these soldiers would either be killed in the pre-invasion barrage or desert their posts in terror. All the first wave of 1,450 American infantry and 96 Shermans had to do was storm in and mop-up the survivors.

The beach *had* to be taken, and the Allied plan looked sound. But, as General Eisenhower had commented in advance of the invasion, plans are everything before the battle, and useless once it starts. Of all the fighting on D-Day, *Omaha* turned out to be the bloodiest.

Sergeant John Robert Slaughter was in the third wave of infantry, approaching the beach at seven o'clock that morning. He couldn't see much of the action ahead of him, hemmed-in and seasick as he was. Slaughter had been pitching on the Channel for three hours and he was so cold his teeth were chattering, his uniform was sopping wet and his helmet was full of his own vomit. He was longing to get out of the boat and start the war. For months he'd been trapped in a dreary training camp near Salisbury, depressed by the weather and English food rationing. Brussels sprouts were a particular bugbear. The sooner the Americans got over to France, he reasoned, the sooner he'd be on a ship home; the 19-year-old Slaughter expected *Omaha* to be a pushover, and to see a German surrender before Christmas.

When they were only a few hundred yards from the shore, the first shells came in. The men still couldn't see much of the beach. It was a dull, overcast morning, and there was so much drifting smoke, the looming bluffs were no more than a blur. Battling with his seasickness, Slaughter noticed the explosions getting closer, throwing up great spouts of water around his landing craft.

"I'm dropping you off here," the British pilot announced to the huddled men. They were still a few hundred yards away from the beach.

"You're taking us all the way in," answered a sergeant at the front of the boat. "We're too heavy to swim that far."

Each soldier was bulging with over 20kg (44lbs) of supplies and special weapons they were expected to carry into France. To make matters worse, they'd been given new combat uniforms soaked in chemicals, to protect them against poison gas. The cloth was as stiff as board and it didn't let air pass through it. They were either freezing cold or sweating, and their battledress was waterlogged and heavy.

"We'll die if we go in there," the pilot protested.

The sergeant drew a pistol from his belt and placed the muzzle to the pilot's brow. "You'll die if we don't."

The pilot took them in. With 150 yards to go, Slaughter peered over the side of his LCA and saw a boat ahead of him taking machine gun fire. Thousands of tracer bullets - flares to guide a gunner's aim - were lancing out of the smoke along the bluffs, ripping holes in the boat's hull and slicing into the water. Further along the shore he saw other LCAs exploding, burning and capsizing under the heavy shelling. This was no pushover.

Suddenly, the LCA quivered as it ran aground on a sand bar. The pilot didn't wait to be asked; he lowered the ramp. Heavy-legged and weak with motion sickness, Slaughter's platoon stirred themselves into action. As they pressed forwards, Slaughter saw that the ramp was seesawing on the waves, lifting six feet out of the water. The first man off hit the surface and sank like a stone; it was still 100 yards to the beach. Frantically, the platoon tried to inflate their 'Mae West' life preservers and rip off their heavy packs as they tumbled out. Bullets were *pinging* off the sides of their LCA, tearing through bodies and packs. Slaughter hesitated on the ramp, watching the waters swirling red with blood beneath him and trying to time his jump. He glanced up at the beach. Where were the DD tanks, to protect them? Where were the bomb craters from the air-strike for them to shelter in? Where were all the men from the first waves?

With his friends dying around him, Slaughter abandoned the ramp, clambered over the side of the LCA and dropped into the icy water. He began floating towards the shore; it would take him an hour to get there, hidden among the corpses rolling in on the tide. There were dead men everywhere; men screaming and crying out for help, men trapped in LCA propeller blades and men on fire. If a soldier shouted or waved his arms, a German sniper would pick him off. Slaughter saw a private shot down on the beach, calling out for a medic. As soon as the medic ran across to him, he was hit by a machine gun burst.

Nothing could survive this carnage. Flaming vehicles, tanks, half-tracks - trucks fitted with tank tracks at the rear to give them more grip - and wrecked LCAs were spread all along the beach. Mortars, shells and bullets thudded into the waves, and snipers shot the wounded as they tried to drag themselves out of the surf. Getting closer to the shore, Slaughter paddled over to an exposed wooden stake and used it for cover until he noticed a mine dangling above his head. He moved across to another post, and studied the chaos around him.

The attack had failed. None of the troops had made

it off the beach, and most had lost their weapons and
equipment and were pinned down close to the surf.
He saw a huddle of men at the shingle bank, trying to
dig themselves foxholes with their bare hands. Even
with the mortar fire raining down on them, they had
more shelter than anyone trapped out in the open.
Slaughter knew he had to get up there to join them,
across a hundred yards of sloping sand. But he was
exhausted, sick and frightened. Slowly, mustering all
his strength, he dragged himself up and got ready to
run...

At 08:30, a navy commander supervising the
Omaha landing gave the order to *retract and postpone*.
Over 50 LCAs, dozens of Landing Craft Infantry ships
- LCIs - each carrying 200 men, and several tank
transporters turned back to sea to circle off the shore,
unable to deliver their cargo because of the disruption
on the beach. General Omar Bradley, head of the U.S.
First Army and senior officer at *Omaha*, could only
peer into the dense smoke and flame from his
command post on *USS Augusta*. When he sent an
adjutant to shore in a patrol boat, the grim report
came back that the draws were still in German hands
and the attackers couldn't get off the sand. Bradley
faced a terrible dilemma. If *Omaha* turned out to be
another Dieppe, he risked sending thousands of men
to their deaths - 55,000 soldiers were scheduled to
land on *Omaha* that day. But, if he ordered a retreat,
the troops already landed would be captured or
massacred at the waterline. The landing force could be

transferred to *Gold* or *Utah*, but that would leave a 40km (25miles) hole in the Allied front and the whole invasion might be threatened. Bradley decided to wait, hoping that some of his men could get past the German defenders and open the draws. At the back of his mind, he must have wondered how all the Allies' careful planning had gone so badly wrong.

When the German gunners had first spotted a fleet of enemy ships, on course for La Plage d'Or, they'd thought it must be some kind of elaborate trick. Perhaps the landing boats were empty, or booby-trapped, a diversion for a raid happening further along the coast. Surely the Allies weren't going to attempt a frontal infantry attack against well-armed veterans?

Allied intelligence assumptions about how well - or how badly - *Omaha* was defended had been seriously flawed. Contrary to all their reports, the Germans on *Omaha* were not feeble old men and disenchanted POWs. They were able soldiers from 352nd Infantry Division, who had been massing along the Calvados coast for several months. The 352nd did have some Ost battalions recruited from former POWs, but the bulk of the division was made up of seasoned combat troops. They were gritty trench fighters, having participated in Hitler's long, tactical retreat across Russia.

When the bombers came, the Germans ran to their bunkers. They needn't have bothered. Of the mass of explosives dropped, only three bombs fell on the beach fortifications, causing little damage. The cloudy conditions and strict orders to leave a safety-gap between the target and the flotilla of landing boats had made the bombardiers unduly cautious. Their explosives fell into the *bocage*, miles inland.

The naval bombardment was more effective. Earth and masonry fell from the bunker ceilings, as massive shells drilled into the bluffs. Soldiers were deafened and stunned by concussion from the blasts, and there were casualties among the platoons stuck in the trenches. But even though some shells scored direct hits on the concrete fortifications, they couldn't destroy them. The architects of the Atlantic Wall had done their job well. Only a lucky hit through a gun slit could smash one of the 15 bunkers - the Germans called them *resistance nests* - which overlooked the beach and the draws.

Most of the DD tanks, which might have opened the draws, sank in the channel. The rocket attack that marked the end of the barrage overshot the bluffs or landed in the water. It killed thousands of fish, but very few Germans. When the dust finally settled, the defenders checked their guns and waited for the infantry to arrive. Rommel had ordered them to hold the Allies on the beaches; they were confident they would not disappoint the Field Marshal.

Sergeant Slaughter was a very tall man. He knew every machine gunner and sniper in the bluffs would see him when he staggered up and started running for the shingle bank. But he also understood that if he stayed on the beach he would die. Remembering his infantry training to crouch and zigzag under enemy fire, he forced himself into a run.

It felt like the longest sprint he'd ever attempted. His clothes were still wet and heavy, and halfway across he stumbled into a long dip or stream of water in the sand, known as a *runnel*. (Another consequence of the tidal movements on *Omaha* was that long runnels formed along the beach, deep enough to swallow a man.) Slaughter lost his balance, recovered, and kept his feet moving. All around him the sand whispered under the impact of machine-gun bullets. But Slaughter made it to the shingle.

After he'd caught his breath, the first thing he did was to spread his raincoat over the ground, so he could put his rifle down and clean the sand out of it. The coat was full of bullet holes, as was his pack. He fumbled to light a cigarette, but his hands were shaking too much to hold it to his lips...

There were hundreds of men with Slaughter, trapped in a line at the shingle bank. They had lost most of their weapons, and their commanders were dead. (Officers had led their platoons off the boats, and were the first to be shot down by snipers.) Without leadership, some of the men lay frozen with fear. But there were other soldiers there who knew what had to be done. Units from the 5th Rangers were already moving up the bluffs, picking their way through minefields and blowing holes in the barbed wire with *Bangalore* torpedoes (long pipes stuffed with explosives).

Brigadier General Norman Cota was one of the few commanders still on his feet. He marched from one group of crouching infantry to the next, urging them to get up over the shingle and start fighting. When he came to some Rangers he made his famous remark: "I'm expecting the Rangers to lead the way off this beach." *Rangers Lead the Way* subsequently became the regimental motto. Another inspirational leader was Colonel Charles Canham. He advised one group of terrified soldiers: "They're murdering us here, let's move inland and get murdered."

The U.S. Navy had seen the troops' predicament before the bluffs, and they did not fail them. At 10:00, Rear Admiral Bryant ordered his destroyers to get as close to the beach as possible to offer help. Some of the ships cruised to within 900m of the shore, scraping their keels along the sea floor as they fired broadsides into the German fortifications. Although the concrete was bombproof, the ground beneath it was not. The battleships gouged the resistance nests out of the earth, ripping them from the bluffs. This sight was met with cheers from the American infantry.

At the same time, the landing craft resumed operations. They had to ram their way through some of the beach obstacles, but enough of them made it through to offload the tanks, troops and other vital equipment. A 'tankdozer' - a bulldozer covered with protective steel plates - finally forced a passage through the first draw, *Easy 1*. By 12:00, vehicles were rolling off the beach, battling their way out of the bluffs and on to the villages inland.

Sergeant Slaughter was in France to fight: as soon as he'd rallied his energies, he joined a small group of soldiers making a rush at the shingle bank. They clambered over through a gap in the wire and began inching their way towards the bluffs. There was a sergeant up ahead, leading a column of men into the mouth of a draw. Slaughter tagged onto the end of their line. Pinned down by shells and machine-gun bullets, one of the column spotted a German mortar battery, hidden among some bushes and scrub above them. It was pounding away at the LCAs in the surf.

Slaughter watched as the sergeant in charge retrieved a radio-backpack from a dead soldier and cranked it into life. When he'd made contact with a warship gun crew, he gave them some map coordinates and waited to see what would happen.

There was a flash from the decks of *USS Satterlee*. A shell from one of her guns ripped into the bluffs just to the side of the mortar battery, blasting clumps of earth onto the beach. The sergeant adjusted his coordinates and the next salvo was a direct hit. The sight gave Slaughter a great surge of confidence. At last, the attack was going their way. Reinforcements were pouring in behind them on the beach and already some of the German defenders were trying to surrender. Slowly, fighting every step of the way, the column started working their way into the draw...

John Slaughter was one of 34,000 troops who landed on *Omaha* that day. Around 2,000 of them were killed or injured in the assault - but the Americans took and held the beach. Slaughter was awarded two purple hearts and a bronze star for his war service, and later helped to establish the National D-Day Memorial in Bedford, Virginia. This small town had sent 34 of its young men to France. Nineteen of them died in the first attack wave, and three others were killed during the battle for Normandy.

The bicycle commandos

Major Patrick 'Pat' Porteous might have experienced a sense of déjà vu as he approached Sword Beach that morning. He was only 26 years old, but already a veteran of one daring amphibious attack against the Germans: he had been at Dieppe in August 1942, a captain in the British Commandos. His team of 252 soldiers had been ordered to demolish a gun battery overlooking the port.

After a night spent creeping through minefields and evading patrols, they made a frontal assault on the position. Porteous was shot through the hand and arm but still managed to lead a bayonet charge against the 250 German defenders. He was the first man to reach the battery, where he was wounded again in the thigh. Although he was weak with loss of blood, Porteous supervised the demolition of the fortifications before passing out. Two months later, he received the Victoria Cross for gallantry, telling a throng of waiting journalists outside Buckingham Palace: "I was just lucky."

Seven miles out from the Normandy beach, Porteous looked around at the soldiers he was accompanying into battle. Individual commando units were split into ten troops, each holding around 50 men. Scores of troops had gathered for the Sword offensive, in support of the British 3rd Infantry Division. The massed commando force was called No. 1 Special Service Brigade, but it was a strikingly diverse body of men: battle-hardened Scots, Royal Marines, German Jews from X-Troop and Free

French Commandos who had put in a special request to be first off the boats that morning. Every one of them had completed the arduous training course that earned them the right to wear the regiment's trademark green beret. Despite their differences, they were all commandos.

From across the waves, Porteous thought he heard the strange, mysterious wailing of a set of bagpipes. Brigadier the Lord Lovat, senior commander of the troops, had ordered his piper to play his men ashore...

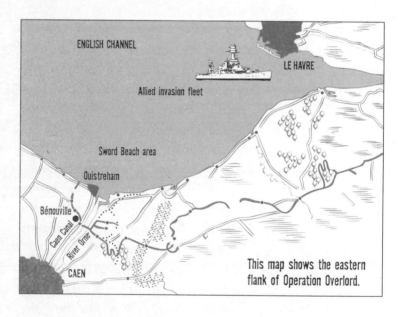

ENGLISH CHANNEL

LE HAVRE

Allied invasion fleet

Sword Beach area

Ouistreham

Bénouville

Caen Canal

River Orne

CAEN

This map shows the eastern flank of Operation Overlord.

Sword Beach was an 8km-wide (five miles) ribbon of sand that marked the eastern flank of the Normandy landings. Commander Montgomery gave General Sir Miles Dempsey's British 2nd Army the task of taking it, along with *Gold* and *Juno*. Dempsey sent the British 50th Division into *Gold*, the British

3rd Infantry Division to *Sword*, and ordered the Canadian 3rd Infantry Division to tackle *Juno*.

Since the close of the Second World War, people have argued about what Montgomery's strategic ambitions really were for D-Day. He must have been hoping to link together all the Allied beachheads and push his forces several miles inland before nightfall. But was he also expecting to seize the ancient town of Caen, 15km (10 miles) south of *Sword*, a vital strategic gateway to Paris? This is a question that has fired many debates since the War.

Major Howard's raid on *Pegasus* bridge and the targeting of British 6th Airborne units to the east of Caen suggest that Montgomery thought he could snatch the town from right under the enemy's nose. If his infantry punched a hole through the German defenders at Ouistreham, the beachside town at the eastern end of *Sword*, they could make rapid progress across the countryside. The landscape inland from *Sword* was much flatter, more open and less hostile to attackers than the *bocage* country further up the coast.

Supported by units of paratroopers and the commandos, a column of Shermans could be rumbling into Caen by the late afternoon of D-Day. It would have been a spectacular victory for the British Commander, allowing him to pivot his whole attacking force around Caen to threaten Paris. But nothing is as unpredictable as war, and generals rarely get what they wish for.

Knowing this as he did, Montgomery waited

anxiously for H-hour to come on *Sword*, at 07:25 on June 6, 1944.

Major Porteous saw the explosions and smoke shrouding the coastline as his 200-man troopship surged forwards on the waves. Gradually, the sounds of battle were drowning out the piper, Bill Millin, and the drone of his bagpipes. The men were cold and sick, bailing water and expecting to sink any moment on the heavy seas. When they were still a hundred yards from the beach, their boat suddenly ground to a halt, leaving them to wade ashore, up to their waists in icy water. Wading would have been easier if they hadn't been under enemy fire and weighed-down by their weapons, spare ammunition, blankets, food, ropes - and everything else an invader might find useful.

Corporal Peter Masters, a Viennese Jew from X-Troop, and each of his fellow commandos, had an extra burden. They had been issued with bicycles for getting across country and they were supposed to carry them over their shoulders as they struggled through the surf. Masters cursed his load all the way to dry land - and this was only the beginning of his ordeal with the two-wheeled contraption.

There was a grim spectacle waiting for the commandos as they neared the beach. Crouching among the floating bodies of dead soldiers, two survivors from an earlier attack wave were slashing at the surf with their spades. Masters couldn't guess what they were trying to accomplish, until another commando told him they'd been driven crazy by the horror of seeing their friends killed around them. "They're digging foxholes," he whispered, "digging in the water."

Masters never discovered if the men were indeed insane, or if they had some other purpose.

The commandos had been ordered to get off the sand as soon as possible and to filter inland on their separate missions. If all went to plan, they were to gather at *Pegasus* bridge and reinforce the British paratroopers there.

Sword was a narrow beach, with no high bluffs or natural obstacles for the defenders to exploit. Where the low dunes stopped there was a concrete sea wall, and then the town of Ouistreham began. Porteous could already hear gunfire and grenade explosions echoing from the suburbs, as the British infantry fought through the streets. Ouistreham had no fixed fortifications around it other than the wall. The Germans had been hoping to stop the Allies at sea, by blasting them with their huge gun emplacements at Le Havre and Merville. But British paratroopers had already smashed their way into the Merville battery and destroyed its guns, and Le Havre was occupied for most of the day, trading fire with *HMS Warspite*, a First World War battleship, but they never hit her.

The only other means of defending *Sword Beach* were the usual resistance nests, an anti-tank ditch and a patchwork of minefields, extending between the dunes. Some commandos sprinted across them, hoping for the best. Another unit inched along a wire fence that ran between two minefields, reasoning that the Germans couldn't lay their mines right up to the posts. But most of the commandos waited for their engineers to mark a safe path with their flags - or stood back and let a tank with special mine-clearing apparatus do its business.

The British Army loved gadgets, and on D-Day they unveiled a whole series of quirky inventions designed to make short work of the Atlantic Wall. They were particularly fascinated by the potential of customized tanks. It was the British who funded the prototypes of the DD swimming tanks, driven largely by the enthusiasm of an 'experimental' engineer, Montgomery's brother-in-law, General Sir Percy Cleghorn Hobart. When Hobart unveiled a whole series of Churchill tanks adapted for special tasks in Normandy, they were immediately nicknamed *Hobart's funnies*.

Although they might have looked ridiculous, the British infantry were right to admire the funnies: they were lifesavers. The *crocodile* was a flame-thrower tank that towed its own drum of incendiary fuel. A *bobbin* had a great roll of canvas bolted to its front hull; the tank laid a thick carpet over barbed wire or swampy ground for soldiers to cross. Other tanks carried long bridge sections to drop over ditches. The *flying dustbin* was a demolition charge fired from a huge mortar that replaced the tank's main gun. But the most useful of the *Hobart's funnies* was the flail tank, or *crab*.

The bicycle commandos

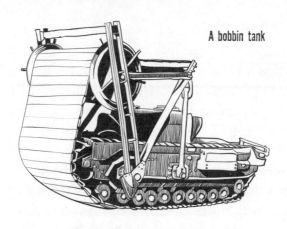

A bobbin tank

A flying dustbin

A crab tank

The front of a Sherman was fitted with a spinning drum, which looked like a tree-trunk, to which dozens of chains were fitted. When the drum was connected to the tank's engine, it started spinning and the chains flailed at the ground. Hobart demonstrated the *crab* to assorted military bigwigs at his BIGOTS-only testing area in East Anglia. They were impressed. And so were the German defenders on *Gold* and *Sword*.

Several tankers reported seeing German machine gunners leap up from their positions in amazement as soon as a *crab* was disgorged from an LCT. The tank growled up the beach, chains tearing at the sand like the hooves of a maddened bull. Every landmine in the vicinity would detonate, and a platoon of soldiers would follow closely behind.

The Americans thought the DDs were a good idea, and worked them into their plans, but they politely refused the other *funnies*. They weren't keen on taking bicycles to France either - unlike their British commando allies.

As soon as a *crab* had cleared the minefields, Porteous and his commandos charged the beach. But MG-42s and mortars were still firing from the dunes and around a quarter of the major's troop of 100 men was killed or injured in the assault. They dropped smoke canisters to confuse the enemy gunners, and one commando destroyed a pillbox with a well-aimed grenade lob. He was later awarded the Military Cross.

While other commandos headed for their assigned targets in Ouistreham, Porteous and his men worked their way along the beach wall, making for a German gun position. They were armed with plastic explosives and had been ordered to demolish the emplacement.

But, as they jogged towards the guns, they were still coming under enemy fire. At one point, Porteous was running past a cottage when the owner burst out and begged the commandos to help his wife who'd been injured by a bomb blast. Before he could answer, Porteous heard the familiar screech of a mortar shell. He shouted a warning to the Frenchman and threw himself to the ground. When the major looked up he saw the man's head rolling along the road.

Moments later they reached the gun emplacement. But the whole site was deserted; the Germans had dragged their guns inland, away from the danger of Allied bombing. Before Porteous could muster his men for the next stage of his mission, one of the commandos was hit by a sniper bullet. A small group of Germans was firing from the top of a high, medieval tower set in the heart of the fortifications.

Porteous was enraged and ordered his troop to surround the tower. He guessed that the Germans were artillery spotters who had been left behind to provide accurate target coordinates for their gun teams, via a radio or telephone connection. Try as they might, the commandos couldn't get close to them. The walls of the tower were too thick to be demolished with a PIAT or explosive charge, and its ramparts too high for any grenade or flame-thrower attack. Access to the roof was by a single twisting staircase set in the middle of the building.

When one commando rushed at this stairway, dodging rifle shots from above, the Germans dropped a grenade and killed him instantly. Porteous had been best man at this soldier's wedding only a few months earlier. But, although he wanted to avenge the loss of his friend, he gave the order to break off the attack. He realized the tower was impregnable and it was essential to join up with the paratroopers at *Pegasus* bridge, 5km (3 miles) inland, as soon as possible. The commandos had to endure the taunts of the spotters as they withdrew and, within a few minutes, they were being shelled by the same guns they'd come to destroy.

While Porteous and his troop were leaving the coast, Peter Masters struggled onwards with his bicycle. He was crawling along a muddy ditch towards his troop's assembly camp, on the edge of a large forest. There were Germans in the woods, and they were taking pot shots at the bicycle commandos. Masters discovered that the only way to keep hold of his precious two-wheeler was to steer it before him, upright and in full view of the enemy. The Germans must have hooted in laughter at the sight of such antiquated technology, and trained their fire on the ditch. Masters breathed a sigh of relief when he saw a couple of Shermans rolling over the brow of the hill to rescue him. As they raked the tree line with machine-gun bursts, he jumped to his feet and made a run for it, arriving safely at the camp.

All X-Troop commandos were bilingual German and English speakers and many of them had other

European languages too. Because of this they were sometimes appended to other troops, to assist with the interrogation of enemy prisoners. Masters had been sent to the assembly camp to work as a translator, but he got off to a bad start.

Lord Lovat had been strolling about with a walking stick and complimenting his piper on his playing technique when Masters arrived. The eccentric commander immediately summoned two swarthy POWs for questioning.

"Find out where their heavy guns are," Lovat asked Masters dryly.

But the two prisoners only shrugged and yawned as Masters quizzed them in his best German. He assumed they were either deaf or tight-lipped, as they wouldn't utter a single word. But a quick examination of their papers revealed they were from an Ost battalion: one man was Russian, the other a Pole.

"Well, then," Lovat snapped at Masters when he heard his report, "don't you speak any Polish?"

Masters had to admit that he didn't. However, he remembered that Poles were taught French at school, so he began questioning the men in that language. But Lovat was fluent in French and wasn't impressed by Masters' feeble performance. He immediately took charge of the interrogation, sending an embarrassed Masters to join another troop which was about to move forward to *Pegasus* bridge.

Masters plodded over to where the troop had gathered and spotted something over a hedgerow that made him cry for joy: an asphalt lane. At last, he could take to the open road. The bicycle he'd been cursing for the last few hours was suddenly a blessing. Dozens of commandos - all armed to the teeth and with blackened faces - formed into a phalanx of bike-riders, pedalling their way towards the enemy. But Masters' country ride was soon interrupted. As he approached the village of Bénouville, an MG-42 coughed into life, catching one of his fellow commandos in the chest and killing him instantly. The troop took cover in some thick undergrowth at the side of the road.

Masters hadn't been getting along too well with the commander of the troop, a Captain Robinson. He had the impression that Robinson and his men thought he was an interloper, and didn't want anything to do with X-Troop. Masters had a very thick Austrian accent. (His cover-story for curious civilians was that he'd had a domineering German nanny.) He felt rather self-conscious among Robinson's tightknit troop, who had been in combat together in North Africa. So he was surprised when the captain called him forward and asked him to go on the crucial reconnaissance mission into the village.

"Of course, sir," Masters replied, happy to have a chance to prove himself. "How many men should I take with me?"

"It's better if you go alone," Robinson answered.

Masters was a little puzzled. "Should I push through these bushes and circle around the town then, sir?" he asked.

"Just walk down the road," Robinson suggested.

"See what's going on."

Masters didn't flinch, even though he now realized the commander just wanted to use him as bait to see where the machine-gun post was hidden. Instead of sending a member of his trusted troop, Robinson was giving the job to the new boy.

Without a second's hesitation, Masters got to his feet and started pacing along the lane towards the village. He never considered refusing the order; instead, he racked his mind to come up with some kind of self-preservation scheme. With no idea of the numbers or whereabouts of the enemy, he decided to risk everything on a bold hoax.

"Right then," he screeched in German, striding up to the village. "I've come to discuss the terms of your surrender. My division has you completely surrounded, so put your hands up and come out."

Not far behind him on the road, Captain Robinson must have been gaping in amazement.

"Send out your senior officer," Masters went on, undaunted by the silence. "If you behave well, you can expect to be treated with mercy."

Masters waited, expecting a machine gun to cut him in two at any second. But nothing happened. Perhaps the defenders thought the commando was a madman, or were chuckling too much to shoot him down? Suddenly, a German jumped out from a behind a low, stone wall and pulled the trigger on his Schmeisser. Masters dodged the burst, rolled to the ground and lifted his Thompson sub-machine gun to shoot back; but the gun jammed. Before his German opponent could correct his aim and finish him off, there was a scream from the commandos at the top of the road. Robinson had no doubts about his man now; he ordered a bayonet charge and the commandos stormed the village, lobbing grenades and firing Bren guns as they came.

At 12:00 on June 6, Masters and his new troop arrived at the western end of *Pegasus* bridge. Porteous and his men joined them only minutes later. The paratroopers in their maroon berets shook hands with the Green Beret reinforcements, and when Lovat arrived he was greeted with a cheer. He marched across the bridge to the sound of his beloved bagpipes, despite the presence of several enemy snipers.

By the afternoon of June 6, Montgomery's plans for the eastern flank of the Allied invasion were all in place. The British 6th Airborne Division and No.1 Special Service Commando had joined forces at the important bridges over the River Orne and Caen Canal. *Sword* was almost secure, and the British infantry and tank battalions that had landed there were only 6km (4 miles) short of Caen. But, for Montgomery, it was a town too far and too hard to capture. An army of 30,000 British soldiers came ashore at *Sword* that day, but they still weren't strong enough to win Caen for their general.

At 16:00, 98 tanks from 21st Panzer Division rumbled out of Caen and launched a devastating counterattack against the British. Supported by the crack German infantry of 192nd Panzer Grenadiers, they had battled their way to the seafront by 20:00. Montgomery's army was cut in two, and had to fight hard to defend the beachheads at *Juno* and *Sword*. By late evening they'd crushed the German attack: 54 of the panzers were destroyed and there were heavy German casualties. But Caen was suddenly out of reach, protected by a defensive ring of artillery, panzers and more Grenadiers.

It would be six weeks before Montgomery had the satisfaction of seeing the Union Jack fluttering above the city. He later claimed that it had never been his intention to send his army so far into France in the opening days of the invasion. The British flank, he said, was designed simply to hamper and distract the best units of the *Wehrmacht* from the planned American advance through western Normandy.

The failure to take Caen on D-Day may still be a matter of dispute, but the bravery of the soldiers who landed on *Sword Beach* is beyond any doubt.

Tiger on the loose

The British soldiers spilled out into the sunshine, leaving their tanks parked in formation at the side of the road. It was just before 09:00, June 13, and they'd been pushing hard since dawn. Now it was time for a cup of tea and some breakfast. The men chatted and joked, despite the fact they were in hostile territory, miles behind enemy lines. These were confident, combat veterans, and their vehicle column had met little resistance as it rumbled through the French countryside.

Perhaps the Germans were too tired and demoralized to fight, and had all gone home? This was certainly the opinion of the locals, who had come out to cheer their liberators when they passed through the little town of Villers-Bocage. They hadn't seen the enemy for days. The British soldiers could still hear them celebrating, a mile or two to the south. There might be some drinking and dancing later, if the commander decided to make camp outside the town. He was up at the head of the column, holding an officers' meeting to discuss the unit's next move.

While the tank crews lazed in the meadows, Sergeant O'Connor was in a half-track troop carrier, motoring up to join his commander. He leaned back in his seat, enjoying his morning ride, when a flicker of movement at the edge of some woods caught his eye. Something big was emerging from the trees. O'Connor was already shouting into his radio microphone as a huge Panzer MkVI broke cover and roared into the open.

"Tiger, Tiger," he cried, "coming right at us."

The next instant, O'Connor saw a flash from the panzer's powerful gun and felt the earth shake as one of his column's Cromwell tanks exploded into flames...

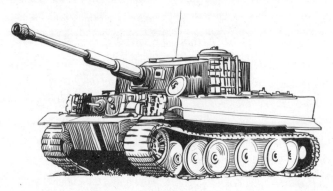

A Tiger

By D-Day+1, the Normandy invasion was up and running, with most Allied commanders agreeing it had been an unprecedented success. Casualties were much lighter than expected and, apart from the bloodshed and delay at *Omaha*, the Atlantic Wall had crumbled as they'd hoped. Some key potential targets - notably the town of Caen, 16km (10 miles) inland from *Sword* - had not yet been taken, but Eisenhower and his generals had landed a fighting army inside France, only a few hundred miles from the German heartland. Supplies, tanks and troops were pouring through the beachheads.

Meanwhile, the Allies' undisputed supremacy in the skies made it dangerous for the Germans to move about in daylight, and hampered their efforts to bring up reinforcements from eastern France. As the Allies' opening gambit in their fight to smash Nazi Germany, *Operation Overlord* was a startling achievement.

But, during the first week of combat, some of the D-Day euphoria began to wear off. For months the men had been psyching themselves up for the challenge of the landings, but now they were expected to fight. Canadian troops around *Sword* resisted a savage counterattack from the zealous Nazis of 12th SS Panzer Division on June 7. This division included fanatical former members of the Hitler Youth, many still in their teens. The British attacking Caen were still struggling to overcome 21st Panzer Division and on June 9, Panzer Lehr, made up of perhaps the finest tank soldiers in the *Wehrmacht*, arrived from Le Mans to bolster the German lines.

Due to their confused command structure and being caught completely off-guard, the Germans had lost crucial momentum for any chance of immediate counterattack on June 6. But now it was the turn of the Allies to watch their troops get bogged down. Their eastern offensive around Caen became a blood-soaked and bitter standoff, as soldiers fought among the maze of hedgerows, small fields and orchards that made up the *bocage*. The corpses of men and animals were littered everywhere, until the smell of rotting bodies hung in a foul cloud over the battlefield. Infantrymen lived with the constant fear of sudden mortar, machine gun or artillery attack. Snipers, PIAT squads and German tank-destroyer teams equipped with *Panzerfausts* - a more powerful version of the PIAT - stalked the shady lanes.

Anxious to get his army moving forward and avoid a stalemate, Montgomery came up with a plan to encircle and crush the Germans defending Caen. He sent elements from his old Eighth Army African units to outflank them; the 51st Highland Division went to the east, and the 7th Armoured Division - the famous 'Desert Rats' - went to the southwest. The 51st couldn't break through the German lines, but on June 12, 7th Armoured found a clear route through the *bocage* towards the village of Livry. They were delayed by a Panzerfaust attack on some of their lead tanks, but by the morning of 13 June they'd penetrated as far as Villers-Bocage. Leaving a strong force of tanks and infantry in the town, A Squadron trundled up a long, straight road to Point 213, a strategic hill about 3km (two miles) to the northeast. From here, the squadron was only 24km (15 miles) southeast of Caen. Montgomery's best batsmen - as he described them - were poised to surprise Panzer Lehr from the rear.

If the British tankers had known who was watching them from the shelter of the nearby woods, they wouldn't have been lounging in the grass, sipping their tea. SS-Obersturmführer Michael Wittmann, a 30-year-old tank commander, was studying the column through his field glasses. Wittmann was tired and needed a rest - as did his six Tiger tanks. He had been on the road since June 7, leading a company of vehicles from Bruges in Belgium towards the action in

Normandy. Passing through Versailles, they'd been attacked by *jabos* - the German nickname for Allied fighter-bomber planes - and the risk of repeat attacks had forced them to travel by night. They had finally arrived to leaguer, or take up position, in the woods during the evening of June 12, their orders to mount a guard on Point 213. Only three of the Tigers were fit for combat; the long road journey had played havoc with the tanks' fragile gear systems.

Wittmann stared at the column greedily, like a cat watching a bird. He knew he was vastly outnumbered and that his men were exhausted, but he also recognized the opportunity that lay before him. The commander had an expert's eye. He was Germany's greatest panzer ace, with over a hundred tank kills to his name.

Born in Bavaria in April 1914, Michael Wittmann's character had been shaped by the same forces that brought the Nazis to power. Wittmann came from a farming family and he always had enough to eat, but the same was not true for his fellow citizens. Following defeat in the First World War, Germany's economy collapsed. In the 1920s, there was a mood of despair and resentment running through the country, which Nazi politicians exploited. They boasted that they could make Germany a proud nation once again. Hitler defied the strict postwar conditions set down in the Treaty of Versailles, and began strengthening his army as soon as he came to power.

Wittmann wanted to be part of this new Germany.

In 1936 he enlisted in the infantry, quickly transferring to the Waffen SS, the Nazi wing of the armed forces.

During training, Wittmann's superiors realized he had a natural talent for handling *panzers*, translated as 'coat of mail' in German. This is a clue as to how some German tank commanders saw themselves: as warrior knights in the modern age. The good-looking country boy had spent years repairing the tractors on his farm and was an excellent mechanic. He was also a skilled hunter, since his father had taught him how to shoot game and track animals in the Bavarian forests. Wittmann was patient and cunning, but always ready to take a risk if he saw a chance for a kill. His ambition, combined with his other skills, earned him a recommendation for officer school. When the war started, he became a tank commander.

Wittmann didn't disappoint his superiors. Battling on the eastern front, he proved to be a daring and brilliant tactician. He also knew how to get the best out of his men. His gunner, Balthasar 'Bobby' Woll, was one of Germany's finest shots, and by 1943 had helped to make his commander a household name. Wittmann understood the debt he owed him. When he was awarded the coveted Knight's Cross medal, he refused to accept it unless Woll received one too.

Striding back through the woods, Wittmann decided on his plan of attack. It was bolder and more dangerous than anything he'd attempted before, and he was only able to consider it thanks to the amazing qualities of the new tank at his disposal - the Panzer MkVI, known as the *Tiger*.

Artillery shelling was by far the greatest killer in both World Wars, but the weapon that soldiers feared most was the tank. And the one they dreaded above all was the Tiger. Russia's T-34 tank was perhaps a better allrounder, and by 1945 the Allies were producing their own formidable vehicles too. But the Tiger terrorized its enemies like no other weapon, right from its first appearance on the European battlefield in the winter of 1942.

It was a massive, intimidating machine, 8m (26 feet) long and 3m (10 feet) high. Aside from its awesome bulk and the shocking roar of its V12 engine, there were two chief reasons for the Tiger's menacing reputation. Its 'telegraph pole' 88mm gun could knock out other tanks from two miles away, and its nickel-steel hull was so thick it was almost invulnerable to any frontal attack. The gun and defensive plating made the tank slow and very heavy, putting enormous strain on the engine and suspension. Tiger breakdowns were commonplace, and repairs fiddly. But, in the hands of someone who knew how to exploit its strengths, the MkVI was a potent killing machine.

Allied tankers shared gruesome jokes about their chances of destroying the new panzer. It was widely believed that it took four Shermans to knock out a single Tiger, and only one of the Shermans could expect to survive the encounter. But the odds were still with the Allies. The engineering required to make a Tiger was so demanding that, while the Allies manufactured nearly 50,000 Shermans, just 1,800 Tigers rolled off their production line at Kassel in Germany. Only a handful of Tigers had arrived in Normandy by mid-June, but to counter the threat they posed, the Allies designed the Sherman *Firefly*. These tanks were regular Shermans that had been fitted with a powerful antitank gun, as long and deadly as the Tiger's. But it was a clumsy weapon, with an awkward firing sequence. And Fireflies were few and far between on the battlefield. Most Allied tankers were expected to find a weak spot in the Tiger's defensive capability, typically in the tracks or the rear engine plates.

Wittmann rallied his crew, climbed up to the commander's cupola of panzer No. 222 and gave the order to advance. He sent his other two functioning Tigers to attack the head of the British column of tanks, while he rolled out of the trees to engage the vehicles parked along the road. Wittmann's one-tank rampage into Villers-Bocage was about to begin.

The British soldiers were already up on their feet, running for cover as Bobby Woll's first shot ripped into a Cromwell tank, blowing it to pieces. The Cromwell was underpowered and underprotected according to many British tankers - and no match for the Tiger's firepower. To make matters worse, the Desert Rat crews were used to Shermans, which they'd had in North Africa. They were still adjusting to the

Cromwell's different controls.

Inside the Tiger, the five crew members were already sweating and covered in dust, locked inside the airless hull. Engine vibration blurred their eyesight, and the noise made it impossible to hear anything beyond Wittmann's curt but calm instructions in their headsets. It took the crew six seconds to load a fresh shell, fix the sights and fire at a Firefly. Woll hit again, and the impact of the explosion pushed the Firefly into the middle of the road. Living up to the Sherman's Ronson Lighter nickname, it promptly burst into flames. The route down from Point 213 was now blocked by the burning tank, while the Tiger howled over the embankment, joined the road and started moving south towards the town.

Wittmann urged his men on as they crashed down the hill, raking a long line of British half-tracks, troop carriers and light tanks with gunfire. The commander knew he had only a few minutes to take advantage of the total surprise of his attack, while the enemy was still dazed. Woll concentrated the 88mm gun against heavy vehicles and the Tiger's MG-42 laced the road with bullets. Most of the British soldiers had already scrambled into a ditch in the fields. They were safe, but the machine-gun fire punched holes in their troop carriers, igniting their fuel tanks. Within seconds, the Tiger was at the head of a long, burning cavalcade of broken trucks, all billowing black smoke and flames. In the panic and confusion, the British wondered if they were under attack from a whole battalion.

At the first road junction, Wittmann saw three

Stuart tanks turning to face him. These tanks were used by army reconnaissance teams because they were light and fast, but their 37mm guns were little better than toy catapults against a heavy panzer. Wittmann's men might have sensed a series of gentle taps on the hull as the Stuarts opened fire, but nothing more. It was a short-lived, if valiant, stand. Woll destroyed the Stuarts one by one as the Tiger throbbed past.

A few yards further on, panzer No.222 charged another group of vehicles milling about on the road, trying to line up for a shot. The 88mm flashed, there was an ear-splitting crack and a Cromwell disintegrated. In all the smoke and dust, one Cromwell backed into the garden of a house to get out of the Tiger's path. Captain Pat Dyas, a spirited Londoner, was its commander. He watched Wittmann thunder past, exposing his Tiger's vulnerable flank at point-blank range. If Dyas had fired, the Cromwell's shell would have punctured the Tiger's hull, but his gunner was on the other side of the garden, answering the call of nature when the attack began.

Cursing his bad luck, Dyas picked up a new gunner and began creeping along the road. He reckoned that if he stalked the panzer from the rear, he might be able to get a shot into its back plates. Keeping his tank hidden in the smoke of the battle, Dyas shadowed the German's advance. It took a brave man to go hunting for a Tiger, and he was soon to get the shock of his life.

Wittmann was too busy charging forwards to pay any attention to the road behind him. Woll destroyed two more Shermans, a half-track and a scout car before the Tiger finally swung into the outskirts of the town, slowing as it approached another road junction. Wittmann and his crew stopped at one end of a long, straight high street. Parked at the opposite end of the street, a few hundred yards away, was a Sherman Firefly, commanded by Sergeant Stan Lockwood. Lockwood had seen the Tiger's advance and its gun flashing as it pulverized A Squadron. He was ready for a fight, and fired at the Tiger's flashing muzzle.

The Firefly shook and was pushed back a few feet by the recoil from its huge gun. Inside, the crew had to cover their ears and open their mouths to protect themselves against the shockwave. Stan Lockwood peered out at the spot where he'd last seen the enemy tank. The panzer was still there, and its gun was aiming towards him.

Like two, heavily-armed gunslingers from the Wild West, the tanks traded shots at one another down the length of the street. As bricks and paving slabs rained down from the shell explosions around him, Wittmann must have realized he was up against something more powerful than a regular Sherman. Before the Firefly could hit home, the Germans were backing away, tracks skidding as they retreated up the hill towards Point 213. Rumbling out of town, they burst out of a cloud of smoke and ran straight into Dyas, who was still tailing them in his Cromwell.

The hapless Brit must have rubbed his eyes in horror as he saw Wittmann's panzer pounding towards him. He fired twice, and saw both shells bounce off the Tiger's thick hull. One return shot from the *Tiger* sliced into the Cromwell, lifting Dyas out of his turret and throwing him 20 feet through the air. He came to earth in another garden. Despite being stunned, he managed to stagger off to the nearest aid-station and lived to fight another day.

Wittmann was now in for a shock of his own. As his Tiger roared up to the last road junction before Point 213, a shell thudded into its tracks and exploded. A British sergeant had managed to gather some of his anti-tank team from the ditch along the road. Although their gun was no more potent than the inadequate Cromwell's, the team had been lucky. Their shell couldn't rupture the Tiger's hull, but it immobilized the tracks. Wittmann's destructive attack was over, fifteen minutes after it began.

Thinking he might be able to recover his precious tank later, he decided not to set its self-destruct explosives. Instead, Wittmann ordered Woll to fire a few rounds of high-explosive, to keep the British occupied, then he bailed out with his crew. Sneaking through the ruined houses at the edge of the village until they reached open fields, the German tankers made their way to the secret headquarters of Panzer Lehr, a château located a few miles to the north. There, they were debriefed and congratulated by General Fritz Bayerlein, commander of the division. The men might even have been treated to a celebratory glass of champagne. Only hours later,

Tiger on the loose

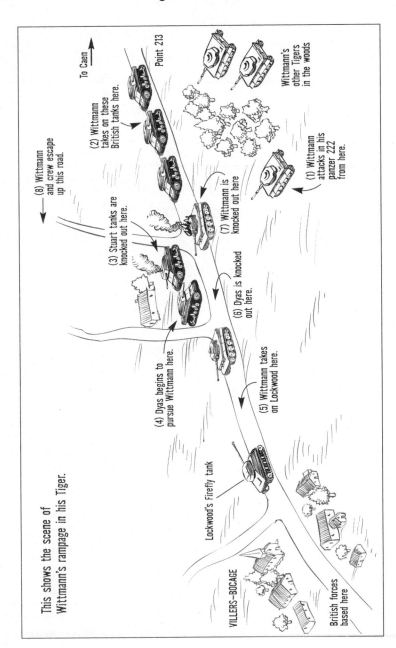

This shows the scene of Wittmann's rampage in his Tiger.

To Caen

Point 213

Wittmann's other Tigers in the woods

(1) Wittmann attacks in his panzer 222 from here.

(2) Wittmann takes on these British tanks here.

(3) Stuart tanks are knocked out here.

(4) Dyas begins to pursue Wittmann here.

(5) Wittmann takes on Lockwood here.

(6) Dyas is knocked out here.

(7) Wittmann is knocked out here

(8) Wittmann and crew escape up this road.

Lockwood's Firefly tank

VILLERS-BOCAGE

British forces based here

while the battle for Villers-Bocage still raged, Nazi radio broadcasts were beamed across Germany, describing the SS lieutenant's daring raid. The Germans quickly sealed any holes in their lines around Villers-Bocage, and by June 14 Panzer Lehr was in control of the town.

The savaging of 7th Armoured by a single Tiger tank shocked Montgomery and the other Allied commanders. Most of the officers on Point 213 had been taken prisoner by Wittmann's two Tigers and a supporting force of infantry. Several other divisional officers were sacked or moved to administrative posts as British generals tried to find an explanation for the catastrophe.

Wittmann's personal tally was startling. In 15 minutes, he'd destroyed two Shermans, six Cromwells, nine half-tracks, five troop carriers, two anti-tank gun units, three Stuarts and one scout car - 25 vehicles in all. On June 25, he was promoted to the rank of SS Hauptsturmfuhrer and flown to a secret meeting with Adolf Hitler. The Fuhrer presented him with crossed swords to be added to his Knight's Cross. Similar to the bar on a British medal, this was one of the highest decorations a German soldier could ever receive.

Wittmann's success was a clear warning to the Allied forces that they had underestimated the fighting strength of the *Wehrmacht*. Every yard and every hedgerow had to be contested against determined opposition. In many cases, the only way to smash the enemy lines was to grind away at the defenders until they were isolated, leaderless and short of ammunition. Even then, some German units showed incredible tenacity, and still managed to launch counterattacks and surprise raids. SS divisions claimed they would fight to the last man. The SS soldiers were determined and ruthless but they were not indomitable.

Learning from their mistakes, the Allies finally prevailed. On August 16, Rommel's successor, Field Marshal Gunther Hans von Kluge, ordered a general retreat from Normandy and the tattered German divisions began their desperate retreat back home.

Wittmann would not be joining them. The slim, ace tank with his confident smile made his last panzer sally on August 8, 1944. His score of tank kills stood at 138, higher than any other panzer officer. But his Tiger triumphs were over. Wittmann and his crew were killed by a Firefly shell, which wiped out their panzer in a grassy field south of Caen. They lay buried in an unmarked grave until 1982, when their remains were discovered and reburied in a German war cemetery at La Cambe.

Out of the dawn

Thousands of soldiers and civilians witnessed the D-Day landings. But, in their memoirs, commentaries, books and interviews, they all seem to share one memory that is more distinct than all the others. It was their first sight of the Allied fleet, 5,000 ships scattered across a stormy sea. When people saw that fleet, they knew they were part of something that would change world history.

On June 6, 1944 the fleet delivered close to 175,000 men, smashing their way through the Atlantic Wall at the cost of thousands of lives. By June 12, the five beachheads were secure and receiving a flood of supplies. On June 27, the Allies took Cherbourg and on July 9 the British finally battled their way into Caen. By July 25, the Allies had landed an army of 1,450,000 fighting men in France, while the *Wehrmacht's* ranks were in tatters; their airforce and navy nowhere to be seen. The German retreat from Normandy was long overdue. Although Hitler's soldiers kept fighting during the relentless pursuit into their homeland, final defeat in Berlin eleven months after D-Day was never seriously in doubt.

The Allies made mistakes. They'd underestimated the difficult terrain of the Norman *bocage*, and at times it looked as though they were losing the energy displayed in their initial attack. But their achievements had been dazzling. In one of the most remarkable espionage coups in history, they had duped the Germans into believing the invasion would come at Calais. Their planning and intelligence work for a mission involving hundreds of thousands of diverse troops was unprecedented. And they met every technical and organizational challenge bravely. It was an amazing and momentous day for the world.

And there was nothing more impressive than the sight of that fleet, looming out of the grey, unpromising dawn...

Glossary

This glossary explains some of the technical, military and other words you may come across in the book. If a word in an entry is in *italics*, it means it has an entry of its own, or is a foreign word.

Allies The countries at war with the *Axis powers*. Britain, the Soviet Union, France and the USA were the main Allied nations.

amphibious Relating to military operations launched on land from the sea.

armada A large fleet of ships or planes.

armaments An army's weapons and *munitions*.

artillery Large, mobile guns firing *shells*.

Axis powers The countries fighting the *Allies*. The main members of the Axis were Germany, Italy and Japan.

BAR Stands for Browning Automatic Rifle, used by the *Allies*.

battalion An army unit made up of a headquarters and two or more companies of soldiers or other smaller units.

battleship A large, heavily armed warship.

bazooka A portable rocket-launcher used as an anti-tank weapon.

beachhead A first landing point for an invasion.

BIGOT Codename for people who knew about the plans for the D-Day operation.

bocage Normandy landscape made up of small fields and high hedgerows, making it difficult to cross.

bunker An underground room, designed to be bomb-proof.

civilian Anyone or anything not part of the armed forces.

commando A soldier trained in special combat techniques.

DD tank A nickname for an *amphibious* tank.

destroyer A warship designed for speed, armed with *torpedoes*, heavy guns, depth charges and even missiles.

DZ The abbreviation for "drop zone" - meaning the area where a *paratrooper* is expected to land.

Glossary

emplacement   A fortified position for troops or guns.

evacuate   To move troops or civilians away from dangerous areas.

Firefly   The M4A4 VC tank, a British version of the U.S. *Sherman* tank, equipped with a powerful main gun.

fusillade   A burst of fire from many guns at once.

fuselage   The main part of a plane that holds the crew and cargo.

garrison   A large military post and the troops stationed there.

Gestapo   The *Nazi* secret state police.

glider   A light-bodied aircraft with no engines, used for transporting troops and *armaments*.

grenade   A small explosive weapon thrown by a soldier.

half-track   A steel-plated military vehicle with caterpillar tracks.

H-Hour   The time when a military operation is due to begin.

Higgins' boat   Another name for a Landing Craft Vehicle Personnel boat, or *LCVP*, named after its designer, A. J. Higgins.

incendiary   A bomb, or fuel, designed to start fires.

infantry   Soldiers who fight mostly on foot.

LCA   The abbreviation for Landing Craft Assault boat, a small troop carrier for *amphibious* landings.

LCVP   The abbreviation for Landing Craft Vehicle Personnel boat, used to carry troops and light vehicles to shore. Also known as a *Higgins boat*.

leaguer   To park a group of tanks in a defensive position.

Luftwaffe   The German airforce.

Maquis   Another name for the French Resistance.

MG-42   A German heavy machine gun, also known as a *Spandau*.

mine   An explosive device hidden underwater or below ground.

minesweeper   Military ship used to destroy *mines* at sea.

misinformation   False information spread to confuse enemy spies.

mortar   A wide-barrelled gun that fires a *shell*, also called mortar.

MTB   The abbreviation for Motor Torpedo Boat, a fast, patrol boat armed with *torpedoes* to use against enemy ships.

munitions   Ammunition, including bullets and *shells*.

Nazi   A member of Hitler's political party.

occupied territory   Land under the control of an enemy power.

Glossary

Operation Overlord   The codename for the D-Day invasion.

Ost battalions   German army units made up of captured Soviet soldiers and refugees from Eastern Europe.

panzer   A German tank or vehicle with a steel-plated body.

Panzerfaust   A powerful German version of the *PIAT*.

paratrooper   A soldier who goes into battle jumping from a plane, using a parachute.

PIAT   The abbreviation for Projector Infantry Anti-Tank, a British anti-tank weapon.

pillbox   A concrete building housing a machine gun, or gun crew.

radar   Stands for Radio Detection and Ranging, a method of fixing the position of an object using radio waves.

Ranger   An American or Canadian *commando*.

reconnaissance   The inspection of an area to gather military information in advance of an attack or operation.

resistance   A secret group of fighters, operating inside an *occupied* country.

sabotage   To damage or destroy something in order to make life harder for the enemy.

salvo   Several large guns firing at the same instant.

sapper   An army engineer, skilled in defusing and clearing *mines*.

Schmeisser   A German sub-machine-gun.

shell   A missile fired from *artillery*, packed with explosive.

Sherman   A U.S. tank, named after a famous American general.

sniper   Someone who takes shots at enemy soldiers without revealing his position.

squadron   A small unit of cavalry, aircraft or naval vessels.

SS   Abbreviation for *Schutzstaffel*, a *Nazi* organization.

storm trooper   A German soldier trained in special combat techniques, specializing in sudden shock attacks.

task force   A group of soldiers formed to carry out a special task.

Tiger   Another name for the German Panzer Mk VI heavy tank.

torpedo   A cylinder-shaped self-propelled weapon carrying explosives, launched from planes, ships or submarines.

Wehrmacht   The German armed forces.

Usborne Quicklinks

For links to exciting websites where you can listen to eyewitness accounts and radio broadcasts of the D-Day landings, read newspaper clippings, follow an animated map and find out more about the Second World War, go to the Usborne Quicklinks website at www.usborne.com/quicklinks and enter the keywords "true stories d-day".

Internet safety

When using the internet, make sure you follow these safety guidelines:

• Ask an adult's permission before using the internet.

• Never give out personal information, such as your name, address or telephone number.

• If a website asks you to type in your name or email address, check with an adult first.

• If you receive an email from someone you don't know, don't reply to it.